The U.S. dollar is on the verge of catast

For the first time in history, the debt o
on Earth, leading the world's largest economy, has been downgraded by
Standard & Poor's to Double AA from a perfect Triple AAA.

U.S. government debt now equals the Gross Domestic Product (GDP).

The 2007-2009 financial crisis appears to have been the first step
toward a deflationary depression that could destroy the savings of three
generations of Americans. We've technically been "recovering" since
March 2009, but despite all government and Fed actions to stimulate
the U.S. economy, unemployment stubbornly remains over 9%.

That is, unless the government's massive cash creation unleashes a wave
of hyperinflation.

Bring on the Crash offers a 3-part process to protect yourself and your
family from these dangers.

Whether you have $2,000 or $2 million, this volume contains all the
resources you need to make sure you weather the coming storm.

This 3 step process is a comprehensive plan to survive the financial
emergencies the US dollar is now facing.

Bring On The Crash!

A 3-Step Practical Survival Guide:
Prepare for Economic Collapse, and Come
Out Wealthier

Richard Stooker

ISBN-13: 978-1466240162

ISBN-10: 1466240164

Disclaimer

I am not a broker.

I am not a licensed securities dealer or representative of any kind.

I am no legal right to sell you securities and I'm not trying to do so.

Nothing in this book is to be construed as a solicitation or offer to sell you securities.

Nothing in this book is to be construed as personal financial advice.

I have no legal right to give you personal financial advice. Even if I was a registered financial adviser, which I'm not, I don't know you or your individual financial situation.

This book is the result of my research and is believed accurate. It consists of my opinions and suggestions.

I'm not making any representations as to how much money you will make if you invest according to the guidelines I set forth — that will depend upon the payouts of dividends and interest of the precise securities you decide to invest in, and nobody can predict the future.

That is part of the problem with mainstream financial advice —
it assumes the future will repeat the past. It doesn't.

Past performance is not indicative of future results.

This book is for education and entertainment. Nothing in this
book is to be construed as professional advice. For that, you
should consult your attorney, accountant or financial adviser.

I am not responsible for the results of your investment decisions.

You must read, think over what I say, make your own investment
decisions and take responsibility for your own life, including
the results of your investment decisions.

Continuing to read this book implies your acceptance of these
terms.

Legal Notice

This document is designed to provide information in regard to the subject matter covered. While attempts have been made to verify information provided in this publication, neither the author nor the publisher accepts any responsibility for errors, omissions, or contrary interpretation of the subject matter.

This information is sold with the understanding that the publisher and author are not engaged in rendering legal, accounting, or other professional services. If legal or expert assistance is required, the services of a competent professional should be sought.

The publisher wants to stress that information contained herein may be subject to varying state, and/or local laws, or regulations. All users are advised to retain competent counsel to determine what state, and/or local laws, or regulations may apply to the user's particular business.

The purchaser or reader of this publication assumes responsibility for the use of these materials and information. The content of this document, for legal purposes, should be read or viewed for entertainment purposes only, and as a work of fiction.

Adherence to all applicable laws and regulations, both federal, state and local, governing professional licensing, business practices, advertising and all other aspects of doing business in the United States, or any other jurisdiction is the sole responsibility of the purchaser or reader.

The author and publisher assume no responsibility or liability whatsoever on behalf of any purchaser or reader of these materials.

In short: The Publisher has striven to be as accurate and complete as possible in the creation of this report, notwithstanding the fact that he does not warrant or represent at any time that the contents within are accurate due to the rapidly changing nature of the Internet.

The Publisher will not be responsible for any losses or damages of any kind incurred by the reader whether directly or indirectly arising from the use of the information found in this report.

This report is not intended for use as a source of legal, business, accounting or financial advice. All readers are advised to seek services of competent professionals in legal, business, accounting, and finance field.

No guarantees of income are made. Reader assumes responsibility for use of information contained herein. The author reserves the right to make changes without notice.

The sole purpose of these materials is to educate and entertain. Any perceived slights to specific organization or individual are unintentional.

Table of Contents

Introduction

I wrote this book to help people who depend on the United States dollar for their economic survival.

That includes almost all residents of the U.S. (I'm sure some people living here have income from foreign countries and therefore benefit when the US dollar goes down) and residents of other countries — expats and others — depending on U.S. Social Security, pensions and investment income.

It's for everybody receiving most of their income in U.S. dollars (which includes myself).

It offers a simple three step process to protect your purchasing power.

I cover all the ways people might think of to hedge their US dollar risk, including some you probably don't know about.

I don't agree every method people use to hedge their US dollar risk is a good idea. I'll make that clear when I write about them. But I cover everything for the sake of being comprehensive.

Economic Gloom and Doom is Nothing New

There are a number of "the sky is falling," "woe is the US dollar" and "profit from the coming crash" books already in the marketplace. Some of them contain useful advice, but on the whole they take a broad look at the economic state of the world and the United States.

I choose not to join them.

First, because such books are not new. I remember reading similar works by Howard Browne and Howard Ruff in the 1970s. I never read The Great Depression of 1990 by Dr. Ravi Batra, but it too was a bestseller. Ten years later he was making money selling The Crash of the Millennium.

I'm Not Chicken Little — But the Sky Might Really Be Falling

The doomsday scenarios never happened. I can't say they never will. I hope not.

Yet I have to admit, as I write, things look grim. Volatility is widespread across the global currency, bond and equity markets.

If things ever get as bad as these guys say, a book won't help you much. You'll need stored food and guns to protect yourself from your neighbors. If you live in a good neighborhood, all of you will need stored food and guns to protect yourselves from the rest of the world.

Anyway, I'm not an expert on growing wheat in your backyard. And I don't want to predict a crash that never happens. I wrote this book to help people for many years to come. I don't want to put a deadline on it or have to explain "yes, the depression didn't happen in 2012, but next year in 2019 it's for sure!" Or 2029!

I'm Writing for Investors Who Need Practical Answers

Secondly, those are "big picture" books that devote most of their pages to convincing you their authors are correct. I'm interested in reading about economic history and theory, but I want this book to be immediately practical for average people and small investors.

You don't need an argument from me the US dollar is declining. That's been a fact of life for over fifty years.

The question now is, what to do to protect yourself now and in the future?

Thirdly, many such books either implicitly or explicitly call for political action. Throw the bums out! Slash the budget deficit! Buy American!

But our government as a whole won't change direction until a lot more Americans are suffering economic pain.

Look at all we went through in 2008 and 2009. Unemployment is still around 9%.

Now Standard & Poor's has downgraded US government debt.

The Republicans and Democrats fought each other down to the

wire of the August 2 debt ceiling deadline. They reached a deal that may help stop us going further into debt, but won't get us out.

The "supercommittee" charged with coming up with a bipartisan plan for cutting the budget by $1 trillion was a predictable failure.

Total US government debt roughly equals the Gross Domestic Product (GDP) of $14.5 trillion.

The US dollar has hit record lows against the Japanese yen and Swiss franc. That's true even though the Bank of Japan and the Swiss National Bank intervened to buy massive amounts of US dollars.

Gold recently hit a high of $1,813 per ounce.

Millions of Americans have lost their homes or seen their home values decline by up to 50%. Same with 401(k)s, IRAs and other investment accounts.

As I write, the Dow is just over 11,000, a point it first reached in Fall 1999. The so-called "lost decade" of the stock market has now lasted twelve years – and counting.

2012's elections are bound to be highly charged.

Are enough Americans hurting enough to elect a president, Senate and House of Representatives devoted to reducing the budget and strengthening the US dollar?

I don't know. And let's face it – we're not yet in half the pain felt by average Greeks, who spent months rioting in the streets but failed to stop the austerity measures imposed on their country.

I hope the US electorate will elect politicians that solve our economic problems before China dictates terms to us the way France and Germany are dictating terms to Greece.

But this is not a political book. And I don't know if we can wait until January 2013 (when the newly elected will take office).

You need to protect yourself and your family.

The Politicians Aren't Protecting You, So You Must Protect Yourself and Your Family

The economic situation of the United States will have to get a lot worse before the general population allows the long term trend of drifting toward socialism — which began a hundred years ago — to change. If we go through a crash such as one being predicted by some, then it may happen. Unfortunately, if there is a drastic economic catastrophe, we could also wind up living under a far right wing or far left wing dictatorship.

The rise of Occupy Wall Street makes matters even worse.

If you wish to "educate, agitate, organize" for fiscal responsibility, God bless you and good luck. But this book won't help you with that.

Also, there doesn't have to be a "crash" for your US dollar purchasing power to be at risk.

It's been declining for many years.

Some of that decline was inevitable. At the end of the World War 2 we were the major world power. But we couldn't expect Europe and Japan not to rebuild. We encouraged and helped them, and that was the right thing to do. And America today is wealthier partly due to European and Japanese products and services.

Now we face economic competition from them, and that's proper — we extol competition.

We're also facing economic competition from China, and that's good. Although they're still an autocratic government that calls itself "communist," in action they've been more purely capitalistic than us since the Gang of Four were thrown into jail shortly after Mao's death.

But the dollar rising and falling because of normal trade fluctuations is one thing.

The dollar steadily falling and falling because we can't control our national spending — that's quite another.

But that's what's been happening for decades.

The US Dollar is Bound to Continue Going Down — Whether It Crashes or Continues a Slower Decline

For decades our government has been following an unofficial "soft dollar" policy to keep the goods and services we produce at a low price so foreigners will buy them.

I said above I don't know whether a dollar "crash" — as predicted by some doomsayers — is ever going to happen.

Maybe it will, maybe it won't. I don't know.

The word "crash" implies a sudden, fast implosion of value.

However, the US dollar has had a prolonged, slow implosion of value since 1971.

So it's happened in forty years rather than overnight.

It's still the theft of our purchasing power, and seems to be speeding up rather than slowing down, which is why so many of us are fearful of the future. I don't know about you, but I plan on living another forty years and more.

And I plan on living well. I don't want a mansion or a BMW, but I do want the security of knowing my dollars will always buy a clean safe place to live, good food and transportation.

I wish I could trust my government to keep my US dollars strong enough, but I can't, so it's up to us to protect ourselves.

Where I'm Coming From

My first book on financial subjects is Income Investing Secrets. So I'm biased toward income and biased against depending on asset market values. I believe you should expect to receive income from all your money except what you keep for everyday expenses in an ordinary checking account.

In Income Investing Secrets I analyze all the common forms of investing: individual securities, actively traded mutual funds, index funds, and Exchange Traded Funds.

I also describe the types of income investments: utility stocks, REITs, Master Limited Partnerships, bonds, and so on.

I don't want to repeat and overlap myself any more than necessary, so just be aware I think buying individual securities is too risky and owning actively traded mutual funds is way too expensive.

I do suggest mutual funds for people who must invest in small, regular intervals. That's because you have to pay a commission to buy Exchange Traded Funds. However, you can also save up your small, regular investment amounts until they add up to enough to buy a round lot (100 shares) of the ETF. Some brokerages allow you to automatically reinvest dividends from stocks and ETFs without charging a commission. Use an online discount broker and your commission will be minimal.

If you insist on investing for capital gains, you should use Exchange Traded Funds or index funds.

Where available, Exchange Traded Funds are my preferred choice.

You should also understand I believe financial markets are unpredictable.

Some economists and finance experts claim that's because they're "efficient" and "rational."

I believe the markets are unpredictable because they're neither rational nor efficient. Markets consist of human beings who buy and sell for emotional reasons. The markets often reflect the internal war between fear and greed everybody with money invested feels.

During bull markets, greed reigns supreme.

Right now, fear has the upper hand.

This goes for not only stock prices but commodity prices and interest rates.

Therefore, never believe anyone who claims they know where the market will be tomorrow or next year. They're either delusional or trying to sell you something you don't need.

It also means analyzing companies, listening to CNBC and drawing charts is a waste of your time.

Put your money into large numbers of investments that pay you to own them, protecting yourself through diversification.

If you need more information on why I prefer investing for income, why I advocate diversification, why I prefer Exchange Traded Funds, and other details about income investments, check out my book Income Investing Secrets.

Take Control. It's Up To You.

I want you to maintain — and increase — your purchasing power.

That's what we're really talking about here. Not whether the US dollar is higher against the yen today or lower against the euro — it's you and your family having what you need and want.

No matter what happens to the world and U.S. economies.

You can't control what the President and the Congress do. You can't control what The Bank of England does. You can't control the Japanese stock market. You can't control the demand for gold in China. You can't control who wins elections in India. You can't control prices at your neighborhood pizzeria. You can't control the speed or consequences of technological change.

But you can arrange your finances so you and your family continue to live well no matter what happens in your city, your country and your world.

So let's get started.

Although this is not a "big picture" book, I have to cover some basics. I can't assume every reader already knows the fundamentals.

Section One

The Money and Currency Big Picture — How We Got Into This Predicament

Chapter 1

What is Money and How Much Is It Worth?

The first step, as always, is to get a firm understanding in your mind of the relevant facts.

When we talk about the US dollar, we're talking about a specific form of money.

And what is money?

One traditional answer is it's a store of value. It's a convenient way of facilitating transactions between people and businesses.

There's no doubt people started out with crude barter systems.

What if I owned three bear skins and you didn't own any?

But today you killed a deer and I couldn't even kill a rat. You want one of my bear skins, so you offer to trade me half your deer for one of my bear skins. I'm hungry, it's summer and therefore too hot to sleep in a bear skin at night, and so I agree.

A week later you decide you'd like to have another bear skin, so you again offer me half a deer.

Only this day I've killed my own deer, so I'm not hungry and turn you down.

Then you offer me three spear heads. Because you're an expert spear head carver, I agree.

Next week you again offer me three spear heads for my last bear skin rug, but I refuse. Winter is coming and I'll freeze if I don't have at least one.

There's no standard "price" for a bear skin. It was up to individuals to negotiate what both found acceptable, which no doubt changed according to circumstances and transient feelings.

At some point, agricultural communities probably decided upon some standard measures. Maybe one horse was worth five head of cattle or a hundred chickens or ten bushels of wheat.

Early Money Was Symbolic of Value But Tied To It

We also know some societies moved on to create actual "money" — something not worth much of anything itself, but used to facilitate trade. Sea shells, beads, and large rocks are examples.

Precious metals such as gold and silver could be used as money more easily than cattle because they were permanent. You couldn't eat them, but they were even more decorative than conch shells.

Judging by the both literal and symbolic roles of precious metals in ancient stories and myths, gold and silver have been synonymous with wealth for thousands of years. This deep emotional bond with them is widespread.

Around 600 B.C., the Lydians first transformed gold and silver into coins.

Much of the world remained on some variation of a gold or silver standard until about 1971.

Actual gold and silver coins did not require "conversion" from one currency into another. A half-ounce gold coin in England was worth the same in France or Russia. Half an ounce of gold was half an ounce of gold. The picture and writing imprinted on it were not important – only its weight.

Gold and Silver are Heavy and Easily Stolen

However, weight is precisely the practical problem with metallic money. It's hard to carry much around.

And it's extremely insecure because it is so widely accepted. There were many robbers and pickpockets waiting for a chance to steal your money.

Therefore, it became common for the wealthy to store the greater part of their precious metals with banks and goldsmiths. They obtained paper receipts for the amount of gold they had on deposit.

These were known as warehouse receipts. They were proof you had gold in storage at a particular warehouse.

Anybody presenting the receipt to the bank could claim the gold, so merchants accepted these receipts in lieu of gold or silver coins.

Because the paper remained easier to use than the actual metal, the receipts traded back and forth while the metal collected dust on a shelf. Everyone accepted them so long as everyone believed the paper was backed by gold or silver.

I've no doubt clever medieval con men managed to forge such receipts. It couldn't have taken people long to figure out, so long as such paper was accepted as money by a town's merchants and tavern owners, all they really needed was the paper. The gold and silver on deposit was a technical detail. The only person hurt by this practice was, of course, whoever tried to use the counterfeit receipt to claim the nonexistent gold on deposit.

Yet, it's a primitive form of inflation. It put into the local economy extra "money" not backed by anything of communally recognized value.

Gold and silver coins became the money of the world. One positive aspect is they were free of any political ties. As I mentioned earlier, gold is gold no matter what (possibly now dead or deposed) king issued the coin.

The nation-state as we take it for granted now is a fairly new historical development. For most of its history, "France" was not a government but a territory controlled by a particular king and people sharing that culture and language. And the territory fluctuated with the outcomes of wars and invasions.

But Isn't Cash Money?

If you're old enough to have read comic books in the 1950s and early 1960s, you may remember the Donald Duck books were significantly different than the usual sloppy junk issued by Disney and others.

They were written and drawn by a man we first called "the good one," and later identified as Carl Barks.

Most of his stories were marvelous entertainments of travel, foiling the Beagle Boys and humor. But I recall one that contains an economic lesson we'd do well to remember.

I don't recall the plot device (an invention by Gyro Gearloose?), but somehow money started falling from the sky all over the globe.

Everybody in the world considered themselves rich.

Except Unca Scrooge McDuck, who was the only one to realize his much beloved tower full of money was now worthless.

Much against their will, he forced Donald and his three nephews to move to a farm and start growing their own food.

In a few months, with nobody working (because they all owned a million dollars), soon there was no food or anything else on the shelves.

There must be some control on the supply of money – some way of tying its supply to the actual production of goods and services – or it becomes just worthless paper.

In essence, the money falling from the sky was hyperinflation – and President Obama and Chairman of the Federal Reserve Benjamin Bernanke are now trying to make America rich again by showering US dollars from the sky.

Many people believe the control tying money supply to the products and services available in the economy should be the gold standard.

I write a lot more about gold in a later chapter.

The Modern Era Elevated the US Dollar to the Status of Gold

In 1944 the major nations of the world met at Bretton Woods New Hampshire and worked out an economic structure for the post-war world.

It was already obvious the United States would be the post-war giant. Europe and Asia were severely damaged by the (still running) war.

We were physically untouched. This was true of Canada and Australia as well, but they have much smaller populations and much smaller economies.

We had huge military machines fighting in Europe and Asia, thanks to huge domestic industrial machines churning out airplanes, guns, ammunition and other war materials.

And everyone knew once Japan and Germany were fully defeated, that productive capacity would be channeled into consumer items.

Therefore, the US dollar was made into the world's reserve currency. In effect, it became a form of gold. The US dollar was pegged to gold at the price President Roosevelt set in 1933—$35 per ounce. The other currencies of the world were pegged to the US dollar.

Therefore, from 1945 to the early 1960s the world's money was extremely stable.

But that couldn't last. The war-damaged countries of Europe and Asia recovered and grew. President DeGaulle of France took delight in demanding gold from the United States even though we were nice guys and forgave France and European countries their war debts. American farmers and businesses exported many products to the rest of the world. But American consumers also began buying imported products, shifting the balance of trade from a huge credit to a (now huge) deficit.

In 1960 Yale economist Professor Robert Triffin testified to Congress about problems caused by the Bretton Woods system.

Spending by U.S. consumers and the government was increasing the currency reserves of other countries.

But the increase in the U.S. government and balance of trade deficits were causing the other countries to lose confidence in the strength of the dollar.

French economist Jacques Rueff predicted a huge increase in the volume of dollars would cause a collapse in the world's economy, causing another Great Depression.

US Budget Deficits Have Been a World Problem for Forty Years

So our current problem (and prophets of doom) is nothing new.

By 1971 the United States was coming to the end of its ability to trade gold on demand for US dollars. According to economist Milton Friedman at the time, the United States government didn't own enough gold to redeem it for all the US dollars in circulation for that $35 per price.

We were officially bankrupt, but of course didn't want to admit it.

In 1971 President Richard Nixon told the world the US dollar was no longer exchangeable for gold.

Since that time, the major currencies of the world have "floated" in value.

I'm not a "gold bug," however. My points are:

1. Money has to be somehow tied to something of intrinsic value.

Paper that cannot be exchanged for food, shelter and clothing is as good as...Confederate money.

2. Money can simply represent something of intrinsic value.

I'll sell you my oranges in exchange for your warehouse receipt, so long as I'm sure I can exchange that warehouse receipt for shoes for my children.

3. In modern history the tie between money and intrinsic value has become so abstract we accept the symbol even without the official backing of gold.

All major currencies are now "fiat money," meaning they're paper not backed up by gold. They are money by government "fiat" – because the government says so, that's why.

In fact, most of our money is now bits and bytes on computer hard drives. No doubt dishonest hackers think if they can add more bits and bytes to their personal bank accounts, what's the harm in it? Who would even notice?

If it weren't for double-entry bookkeeping, nobody would notice.

And don't politicians do the same thing? They spend money that doesn't now exist. They mail out checks by the simple routine of creating a corresponding debt in the government's bookkeeping.

Here's legal tender today, backed by an I.O.U. to China which is backed by an I.O.U. to the future.

Newly minted money spends just as well as cash.

4. Money now represents social trust. I'll sell you one of my widgets when you give me a five dollar bill. That's true even though the five dollar bill is just a piece of paper with no gold backing. And I'll do it because I know I can exchange that five dollar bill for the hamburgers I want to eat for dinner tonight.

Our acceptance of paper money hinges on our trust in the social order created by the government that issued it. Or at least our acceptance of the legal authority and legitimacy of the government which requires it to be accepted.

Even if we don't like the social order, we must acknowledge its existence. Try to walk into an anarchist bookstore and see whether they'll give you their inventory for free. Not if they want to stay in business. Even anarchists must pay rent and buy food.

5. Money is useful within the borders of the political entity that issued it.

The Soviet ruble had no value outside the U.S.S.R. or Eastern Europe. However, inside the Soviet Union people had jobs and were paid in rubles. They traded those rubles for bread and vodka. They had to wait in long lines and there were shortages, but when something was available to be bought, the price was in rubles.

When the US dollar goes down against the yen and euro, your monthly rent doesn't go up. But the price of Toyotas does. Tomatoes at your local farmer's market remain cheap, but the price of fancy Swiss chocolate goes up.

It's partly a matter of trust. It's partly a matter of necessity. It's partly a legal matter. That's why our money says, "This note is legal tender for all debts public and private." Inside the United States we're required to accept it.

6. Foreign currency exchange represents trust between nations in the overall economic system.

We can exchange US dollars for yen for Mexican pesos because we believe we can exchange those pieces of paper for something of value inside those countries.

However, because the currencies of the world are no longer linked to a store of stable value, there are no checks and balances — except other currencies.

7. Paper fiat currencies are just another product.

Products are "worth" whatever somebody else will pay for it.

The US dollar is now worth whatever somebody will pay for it — in yen, in euros, in Swiss francs and so on.

And, as with all commodities, dollars are subject to the law of supply and demand.

The greater the supply, the lower the price.

The greater the demand, the higher the price.

You and I don't control the economies of the United States or the world. Our job is to maintain our purchasing power no matter what happens.

It wasn't always like this.

Chapter 2

United States Money, Past, Present and Future

During the Revolutionary War, the Continental Congress issued printed money to finance the battles. However, to undermine our revolution, the British introduced huge quantities of counterfeit money. In the end, although we won the war, our money was so inflated we still sometimes say something is "not worth a Continental."

Otherwise, early Americans considered gold and silver to be money. The Mint Act of 1792 defined the US dollar as 371.25 gains of fine silver. This was the weight of the Spanish mill dollar. This coin was commonly used in Colonial America and continued to circulate legally until 1857. It wasn't issued by the US government. It didn't have to be — it was silver. It was money.

When the southern states formed the Confederate States of America and withdrew from the United States, they issued their own paper currency. This of course had no value after they lost the Civil War. Even when I was a kid people still referred to "Confederate money" as the ultimate in worthlessness, because it was paper and the political entity behind it no longer existed.

Meanwhile, up North, in 1863 the war stimulated the United States government to issue the first paper currency. These were "gold certificates." Each one promised to represent gold stored by the government and was payable on demand.

In effect, this was a nationwide form of warehouse receipt. People accepted these pieces of paper as money because they were confident it was backed by gold stored by the government.

In the late 1800s there was a political movement in the United States called bimetallism. Basically, to avoid inflation, an 1873 law demonetized silver. New silver mines in the West had greatly increased the supply.

However, the country suffered instead from deflation. This hurt poor farmers and others who had to pay back debts in dollars suddenly worth more.

Silverites wanted the now plentiful supply of silver to be used as money, as well as gold. Gold advocates wanted our money set only to the gold standard.

In 1896 William Jennings Bryan gave a speech advocating bimetallism at the Democratic Party convention that won him its nomination for the Presidency.

He lost the election, but his portrayal of "idle capital" crucifying mankind "on a cross of gold" has gone down as the greatest election speech in US history.

From Gold Certificates to Federal Reserve Notes

In 1913 the United States Federal Reserve was formed, and began issuing "Federal Reserve notes" as paper money instead of gold certificates. This began weakening the close tie of the US dollar with gold.

During the Depression the major nations of the world went off this type of gold standard. In the United States, the 1934 Gold Reserve Act removed "gold" from the wording of Federal Reserve notes.

President Roosevelt made it illegal for individuals to own monetary gold in the United States. Executive Order 6102 signed April 5, 1933 demanded owners of gold turn it in to the government and receive $20.67 in return. Soon after, he raised the official price to $35. In effect, he stole $14.33 per ounce from Americans.

On November 2, 1963 the federal government made our paper money no longer redeemable.

The 1964 issue of dimes, quarters and half-dollars were the last to consist of 90% silver. 1965 half-dollars are about 40% silver.

Since then, we've gone from carrying "silver" in our pockets to "coins" or "change."

The Danger of Not Tying Money to Gold or Silver is Inflation

The more dollars our government puts into circulation through spending and Federal Reserve policies, the lower its value relative to the other currencies of the world.

The more euros and yen those other countries create, the lower their values relative to the US dollar.

That's the danger of excessive government spending.

The more we demand to exchange our dollars for other products priced in other currencies, the lower the value of our dollars.

The more foreigners demand to exchange their currencies for products priced in US dollars, the higher the value of the US dollar.

That the danger of our balance of trade deficit.

There's a lot of talk in the world – especially from China—about removing the US dollar as the world's reserve currency.

Part of this is simple economics. A lot of banks and government treasury vaults around the world are holding billions of dollars. These banks and governments don't like seeing the purchasing power of their US dollar reserves go down every time another balance of payment report is issued or the Congress and the President enact a budget that grows the deficit.

You can't blame them. You and I don't like seeing the purchasing power of our US dollars go down either.

If the US dollar were no longer the world's reserve currency, it's believed, those foreigners would begin spending them like drunken sailors, buying up our assets or trading them for euros.

This would greatly increase inflation in the U.S. economy.

All World Economies are Now Interconnected to the United States

The trouble is, nobody really knows how a US economic catastrophe would affect the rest of the world.

One of the biggest holders of US dollars is China. However, that country wants to continue to receive big checks every month from Wal-Mart. Those checks would go down if U.S. consumers could no longer afford products made in China.

Without the support of US consumers, tens of millions of young Chinese men and women would be unemployed. Without a job to go to every day, they might demonstrate in the streets.

Enough young people in the streets can change governments, as China's leadership well knows. They're afraid.

Now only that, but China – despite its lectures to us on overspending – has a tremendous amount of debt. According to some, it's up to about 90% of China's GDP – not so far from the US debt ratio of 100% of GDP.

Plus, there's the "crowded aisles" syndrome. If investors in one country exchange a billion US dollars for some Manhattan real estate, that's business as usual.

If China, Japan, the European countries and Middle Eastern countries all tried to cash in their US dollars at the same time, the dollar's value would rapidly plummet by 99% or more.

They'd make a quick profit, but the majority of their dollar reserves would become worthless.

They couldn't sell US dollars fast enough to avoid trashing their own supply, and they know it.

There's an old saying: if you owe the bank a thousand dollars and can't pay it back, you have a problem. If you owe the bank ten billion dollars and can't pay it back, the bank has a problem.

If the United States owes world banks $15 trillion dollars and can't pay it back, the entire world has a problem.

And if the United States dollar plunged in such a disaster, that would mean an incredible reduction in world demand for goods, food, commodities and energy.

Nobody Wants to Feel the Pain

Nobody really wants to face up to this predicament.

Certainly not American politicians. President Bush was a big spender and President Obama an even bigger one.

Most people in the United States would resist true governmental fiscal responsibility as strenuously as the rioters in some developing countries put on an "austerity" program by the World Bank.

In the long run we'd all be better off — but nobody wants to live through the bloody (and I do mean that literally) consequences of true fiscal reform.

Nobody in the United States. Nobody in other countries, except — maybe — a few self-sufficient farmers.

Fiscal fitness is sort of like physical fitness. Everybody wants to be strong. Only a few people get up off the couch and regularly exercise.

Now for the good news.

In many ways, we're better off than other developed countries.

Our Unfunded Liabilities Aren't as Big as Their Unfunded Liabilities or, as Someone Else Said: America is the Healthiest Horse in the Glue Factory

Most of them also have huge, retiring baby boomer populations.

European central banks manage the euro more conservatively than the Fed does the US dollar, but European governments have trained their populations to expect a lot more socialism and welfare. On average, Americans are far harder working, adaptive and entrepreneurial.

Many Americans are upset by the existence of welfare recipients. Most Europeans believe governments should pay out welfare checks, and think we're stingy.

Tell Europeans they have to stop wasting so much money on welfare and government jobs and they riot in the streets. Look at Greece.

Portugal, Spain, Italy and Ireland are also in bad shape and could be forced to accept austerity measures in the coming months.

All of this is draining the taxpayers of France and Germany, who are forced to bail out their neighbors. How long before they start rioting too?

The Japanese government has been trying to spend its way out of its recession since 1989. The post-war generation that worked like hell to rebuild that country is now retiring. Most Japanese still work hard, but they're not reproducing quickly enough to replace their dying elderly.

And now they're faced with paying to repair the damage caused by the March 2011 earthquake, tsunami and the dismantlement of four nuclear power plants.

China seems to be the next country in line to economically power the world but, thanks to its old "one family, one child" policy it too is past its demographic peak. Also, it faces the prospect of internal dissension and revolt if it can't keep its population employed.

And it has massive amounts of debt as well, though it's trying to keep the problem swept under the rug.

The developing world is rapidly advancing, but is plagued by political conflicts and instability.

Facing the threat of Muslim fanaticism over Kashmir is a drain on India's economy.

The "Arab spring" will hopefully bring a lot more democracy to that region, but it is creating a lot of instability and uncertainty. Iran beat down its protestors a few years ago, but eventually the modern young people become modern middle aged people controlling society, as the Soviet Union learned.

Much of Africa is embroiled in war, civil war, revolution and corruption on a mind-numbing scale. Hugo Chavez has revived in Latin America the failed policies of Marxism. Even Thailand saw massive political protests.

And while I'm not convinced we're facing extreme climate change, maybe we are. And certainly we're facing ecological pressures, especially in terms of energy. And if we manage the transition to a post-petroleum society, what would happen to the countries of the Middle East which now rely on oil for their economic strength?

My conclusion here is the future is uncertain and full of threats and risks — as it always has been.

Right now the future of the US dollar looks dim, which is why I'm writing this and why you're reading it, but that's not a certainty.

The currencies and economies of the world face a lot of problems which will drive them up and down.

Nobody knows the future.

We don't even know whether the biggest threat we're facing is inflation or deflation.

Chapter 3

The Argument for Inflation, Possibly Hyperinflation

Inflation is an increase in the amount of paper money in circulation relative to the amount of goods and services available for sale in that economy.

If we live on a small island, with two dollars and two coconuts for sale, each coconut will cost $1 each. If we print up an additional eight dollars, we'll have a total of $10, but still only two coconuts to spend them on, so the price of coconuts will rise to $5 each.

We have more money, but in reality the only way to increase wealth is to increase the supply of goods and services.

If we want more coconuts, one of us has to climb up a palm tree and cut some down.

In short, true wealth comes from increasing the production of goods and services, not from expanding the supply of money.

That's easy to see when you talk about small islands with only two coconuts for sale. It's not so clear when we're discussing

Richard Stooker

entire countries.

Printing New Money is Easier Than Cutting Down Coconuts

That's why politicians love inflation. They can use it to buy votes. They can't actually produce true wealth. That's the job of the private sector, and companies want to be paid for what they do. They want to make a profit. Inflation, therefore, makes voters happy.

With the abandonment of the gold standard, governments around the world have yielded to the pressure of their citizens for financial aid by creating additional money.

Without a corresponding increase in goods and services, this simply raises prices for the goods and services already available.

That's partly why inflation has been such a problem. It's grown since World War II, and was a particular problem in the ten years following Nixon's abrogation of the gold standard.

When I worked my first job in the summer of 1968, I was paid the minimum wage — all of $1.25 per hour. Yet I could read a science fiction paperback for sixty cents, watch a new movie for 75 cents and buy a gallon of gas for twenty-five cents.

The United States Federal Reserve and central banks of other countries have gotten inflation somewhat under control. They drastically increased interest rates in 1978. Since then, both inflation and interest rates have trended down to about 2%.

Sometimes the Economy is Contrary

However, there're a lot of indications inflation could go up — a lot.

When the U.S. government spends more money than it takes in (which it almost always does), it's adding to the supply of dollars in the world.

The United States government is now running record high deficits. President Bush was a big spender even before the financial crisis of September 2008 which pushed him and Congress to pass the TARP bailout bill.

President Obama passed the $787 billion stimulus bill in early 2009, and now is proposing a huge budget. And in a few years we'll begin spending a lot more money on healthcare.

Plus we have a huge amount of what are called "unfunded liabilities."

That's estimated Social Security, Medicaid, and Medicare — expenses the government faces in future years.

Where will the money come from?

Our politicians are just assuming the world will continue to buy United States Treasury bonds, accepting our promise to burden future taxpayers with the debt.

They're hoping they're dead or retired when the crash they helped cause hits. They'll still get their pensions anyway.

Creating and spending this money will continue to drive up the world's supply of dollars.

Current politicians are concerned with their re-election, not with the farther future. Most voters are also concerned only with the present.

Future politicians and voters will also try to kick the can down the road. But how big can our national debt grow until it's too big to kick down the road?

We don't know, and everybody is hoping the crisis won't hit... yet.

And maybe it won't. I'm not predicting a crash soon, because I know the "gloom and doom" crowd have been at it since the 1970s. Our debt was at record high levels then, and the rest of the economy in a shambles. And many people didn't think the system could survive for much longer, but thirty to forty years later, here we are.

In the United States, the Tea Party has done a lot of work to reverse this trend. In 2010 they helped to send a lot of new politicians to Washington DC.

In July 2011 they had enough power to force Democrats to agree to spending cuts to match the raising of the August 2 debt ceiling.

They did not get the spending cuts they really wanted. Considering they do not control the Presidency or the Senate – or even the entire Republican party – I think they accomplished a lot.

At least, for the first time in 16 years, significantly cutting the US budget deficit is part of the national discussion.

The US debt ceiling has been lifted many times in the last fifty years without the press paying any attention.

Now, it's at least a national issue.

Inflation is Insidious

The rate of inflation has gradually been going down since about 1982.

It's gone down so much young people today aren't aware of the threat. It's slow. You don't see much effect from last year to this year, and twenty years away is a long time.

Recently the rate of inflation has been around 2% officially. Let's assume that's accurate. It's the rate Chairman of the Federal Reserve Ben Bernanke is on record as supporting.

In 38 years the value of your money has been cut in half.

Sound like a long time?

When you're thirty-eight years old, you're still a young man or woman.

The standard career now runs 44 years from age twenty-one to sixty-five. And many people start working, at least part-time, while still in their teens.

Many people choose to work past the age of 65. In the financial upheavals to come in the future, many people will continue to work whether they want to or not.

If you don't protect the money you save now, it won't be worth much when you really need it.

And that's at the recent rate of 2% inflation — the lowest rate we've seen since I've been alive (since the Jurassic era).

If the predictions of many experts come true, current U.S. government budget deficits and overspending may send the rate of inflation much higher.

Even it doubles to "only" 4%, your money will lose half its value in just 18 years.

Sound bad?

Believe me, in 1980 a rate of 4% inflation sounded like Utopia.

Inflation can — and in the 1970s and early 1980s did — go into double digits.

At 10% inflation your money loses half its value in only 7 years.

How hard do you want to work today for a dollar that will be worth only 50 cents in seven years?

What will happen to American politics in response to that?

The most famous case of hyperinflation was Germany in the early 1920s. People burnt paper bills to cook and heat their homes because it was worth less than wood.

Their democratic government never recovered. Communists and Nazis fought each other on the streets until Adolph Hitler won the election in 1932.

In more recent times Zimbabwe suffered even worse hyperinflation.

The head of the government Robert Mugabe eventually agreed to share power with one of his opponents (though I'm sure human rights abuses continue). And they don't even have their own currency. They use the US dollar, the euro, the British pound sterling and the South African Rand.

The U.S. Government Encourages the Prophets of Inflation

The government releases lots of economic information, but in 2006 it stopped releasing the M3 money supply figures. I don't like to believe in conspiracy theories, but when the government refuses to give out information it once did on a routine basis, it's hard not to conclude the government doesn't want us to know how much the money supply is going up.

Then there's the "official" measure of inflation — the Consumer Price Index (CPI). The problem with CPI is it excludes the rising costs of food and energy. Apparently the government believes we don't need to eat, drive or heat our homes.

It's to the government's benefit to encourage as much inflation as possible as long as it stays "under the radar" so it's not a political issue (as it was in the 1970s).

The government owes a lot of money — $15 trillion. That's $335.3 billion in interest payments — 12% of federal spending.

Thanks to the recent downgrade of US government bonds, US taxpayers will no doubt have to pay higher rates of interest.

Inflation makes that money cheaper. In effect, the government is issuing "counterfeit" money. (Oh, it's "official," of course, but since it's not backed up by an increase in the world's supply of goods and services, in real terms it's as fake as a forged warehouse receipt for gold.)

It works now because of the social trust we have in our money. One five dollar bill is just as good as another. So we accept them all.

If the interest we pay to Treasury bond owners is too low to keep up with the decline in US dollar purchasing power, tough toe nails for the Treasury bond owners. They actually believed that propaganda about US Treasury bonds being "riskless." What a good joke on them!

That is why "communist" China is more concerned about our budget deficit than President Obama was until he was forced to listen to Republicans by the August 2 debt ceiling deadline.

And if the official rate of inflation is lower than the actual rate, that's even better. Government salaries, pensions and Social Security checks are increased every year based on the CPI. If the CPI is lower than the true level of inflation, that saves the government money.

2010 was the first year since the beginning of automatic Cost Of Living Adjustments (COLAs) increasing Social Security, SSI, and federal government salaries and pensions these checks were not raised at all.

They were not raised in 2011 either, and there's talk of not raising them for the next two years even though the law requires they be raised by the official CPI – and nobody yet knows what that will be in the future.

In effect, the government has told seniors, the disabled, its own employees and retirees their cost of living did not go up in 2009 and 2010.

Did your cost of living go up in 2009 and 2010?

Everybody else's did.

Not Everybody Agrees on Inflation

When I was a business student in 1976, I quickly earned a black mark through my eagerness to demonstrate how much I knew. The professor asked what caused inflation. I told him what I've just told you — an increase in dollars over the supply of goods and services.

I could tell from the way the professor looked down at his shoes as though trying to politely hide his reaction to the bad smell I'd just passed I'd done something wrong.

He explained our country's inflation was caused by the oil crisis of 1973.

I don't want to dismiss the negative effects of that oil embargo, but in fairness we can't blame the Arabs for all the economic shocks of the 1970s. Some of them, yes — but far from all.

One of the biggest inflation worries for the United States is not our budget deficit — we're far from the only country which routinely spends far more money than we have — but we'll lose our status as the world's reserve currency or the rest of the world will simply stop buying our Treasury bonds.

Huge amounts of dollars currently exist in government and institutional vaults in Europe, Asia and the Middle East. If their owners were to start selling even ten or twenty percent of those dollars, that would be a huge influx of dollars into our national economy.

Commodities are Subject to the Law of Supply and Demand

Remember, dollars are a commodity. They too are subject to the Law of Supply and Demand.

If the supply goes up because of such selling, the value of the US dollar would go down — way down.

Technically, the world should have found a new reserve currency in 1971 after President Nixon stopped converting dollars into gold. It's a tribute to the United States' economic and military position in the world they didn't. Also to our history of political stability. Only Switzerland has been a democracy with one continuous government for longer than the U.S.

Besides, back then they had no real alternative.

Now, many people believe, the euro is the stronger currency and would make a better choice.

The recently debt problems of many EU countries and street riots have many fearing the euro will be dismantled.

Some have floated the idea of establishing an international standard using a basket of major world currencies.

I believe nobody is in a hurry to change the current system because they can't foresee all the consequences.

The Short Term Pain Would Be Horrific

However, as time goes by, unless the United States gets its economic house in order, pressure around the world will grow to stop depending on the US dollar.

Eventually it will be successful.

And who can blame them? This book is my way of showing you how to stop depending on the US dollar.

For reasons both good (the economic growth of other countries) and bad (our extreme debt), the US dollar is no longer the one bastion in the world of economic and political stability.

When the US dollar becomes just one major world currency, its value in the international currency marketplace will sink.

So How Can We Control the Growth of Fiat Currencies?

If we must tie our currency to something of hard economic value to prevent inflation, but gold and silver are not the answer, then what is?

I don't think anybody except me is even asking this question.

Modern day economists and central bankers believe in the power of the central banks including the U.S. Federal Reserve.

Hard money types keep repeating the gold "mantra."

I don't believe either one is the answer.

Somehow we've got to find a way to keep politicians from spending more money than exists.

Somehow we've got to find a way to tie the value of our currency to something real, concrete and of true economic value.

Something that will go up or down with real economic activity, whose supply goes up or down only in conjunction with the supply of goods and services not because of mining production.

If you think of the solution, write to President Obama and Chairman Bernanke.

I'm sure they really want to know.

Commodities and Energy Markets

One other factor contributing to the fear of greatly increased inflation is the commodity and energy markets.

We're running out of oil — at least, of cheap oil. China, India and other developing countries are growing much faster than we are and they're driving up the cost of energy and commodities.

This is hard to argue against.

Experts have been predicting the "end" of oil since we started drilling deeper than ten feet. Satellites continue to find more reserves. There's lots of petroleum in the oil sands of Canada and the Western United States. We could drill in Alaska and offshore. We have enough coal reserves to last for many years. Yet there's no doubt all these alternatives are more expensive than a simple old-fashioned well in Texas.

We also have huge amounts of natural gas reserves.

China and India together have an incredibly large number of people. Most of them currently live in extreme poverty. It would take huge amounts of energy and building supplies to bring them up to the living standards of Middle Class America. Not to mention other Asian countries, Africa and Latin America.

The more these people and countries develop themselves economically, the more demand for life's basics will increase. When demand increases, prices go up.

Is more inflation inevitable? What about the risk of its opposite — deflation?

Chapter 4

When the Supply of Money Goes Down — Deflation

Other experts believe we're most at risk from deflation, and that would be even worse than inflation.

Inflation is a slow (generally) thief of stored wealth, but deflation can have a huge, nearly immediate impact.

In deflation, prices fall. That sounds good. And in fact, deflation is good for people who have a secure source of income. Unfortunately, it also destroys what people mistakenly believe are secure sources of income.

Deflation is often depicted as a spiral that grows larger, feeding on itself.

It makes it harder for businesses to make a profit, especially those operating on credit. So they lay employees off.

Who then spend less money, slowing the economy down further.

Debtors are punished, because they must pay their bills with money that's now more valuable than the dollars they borrowed. Thanks to rising unemployment and business slowdowns, many cannot pay their debts. This is bad for mortgage companies, banks, stores and other lenders.

If Left Alone, Deflation is Good for an Economy (in the Long Run) by Destroying Debt

The basic purpose of a deflationary period (recession or outright depression) is to wring excess debt out of the system. A credit contraction is part of the process.

That's economic-speak for an increase in personal and business bankruptcies, foreclosures, repossessions, reduced lines of credit, and tighter credit standards making it much more difficult for businesses and individuals to obtain credit.

And that of course puts some businesses out of operation or keeps them from expanding, plus reduces the number of people who can buy cars and houses.

You may have noticed the above paragraphs describe the 2008-2009 consequences of the financial crisis, and that's no coincidence.

During deflation the price of assets falls. From October 2007 to March 2009, stocks dropped over 50%. They've come up a lot in the past year, but are still far from their October 2007 14,000 Dow record.

Everybody knows house prices have dropped sharply, fifty percent or more in some markets.

If you have a large supply of cash, you can find many bargains. Financially strong real estate investors have been out there buying up low-cost houses.

Yet widespread fear of the future can paralyze people. I remember my grandfather saying once he could have become rich during the Depression by buying stock, but his wife wouldn't let him.

During a deflation more people are trying to sell their real estate and cars to unload the debt. More people are trying to sell stocks and other financial securities. More people are trying to sell their labor to make extra money.

Under the Law of Supply and Demand, Increases in Supply Reduce Prices

So all this selling drives prices down even further.

If you have a secure source of income, you can live well. If your grocery bill drops by 5%, you're better off even if your Social Security check remains the same.

But you have no guarantee the government won't decide to reduce or even suspend Social Security checks.

Or the government itself will continue to exist.

Financial misery is widespread. Employees who keep their jobs often find overtime or even regular hours reduced and pay raises scarce. Business owners struggle to remain profitable. Many fail and go out of business.

In the long run, getting rid of the excess debt is healthy for the overall economy, but it's no fun for the people and families affected in the short run.

When people have less money to spend, they spend less money, lowering profits of businesses, which in turn increases unemployment, which means those (former) employees have less money to spend, and so do the business owners, contributing to the cycle.

That's why politicians want to avoid deflation at all costs. No president wants to be the next Herbert Hoover.

How Long Can the Juggler Keep the Plates in the Air?

However, many experts say efforts to avoid deflation just prolong the economic misery and make it greater when the crash finally occurs.

This includes the Federal Reserve keeping interest rates low (which contributes to the decline of the US dollar but helps keep businesses running) and government programs to keep people in houses they cannot afford.

And, of course, the entire superstructure of stimulus and bailout bills passed by President Bush and President Obama.

Politicians simply don't want to pay the political price of deflation.

The circle is now international. As the saying goes, when the United States catches a cold, the rest of the world comes down with pneumonia.

When Money Stop Circulating, Everybody Feels the Pain

When fewer people in the U.S. buy toys made in Thailand, that toy factory has to lay off workers. Those laid off factory workers now cannot take their family to the local McDonald's, attend a Hollywood movie (Thai movie theaters show Thai, Hong Kong and Hollywood movies), or drink a can of Coke. The factory owner cannot afford to buy a new Ford.

This further reduces profits for McDonald's, Hollywood, Coca-Cola and Ford.

And the decrease in local business also leads to the local McDonald's, and the movie theater laying off their employees — so those young people reduce their spending. The soft drink street vendor can't buy as much rice for her children, which means less money for the rice dealer and the farmer.

And so the impact continues to cascade through the world's economy.

Are We Going to Repeat Japan's Experience?

Some experts believe the United States is in danger of a slow economic, deflationary period similar to what Japan has been in since its stock market crashed in 1989.

There are signs of prices and wages falling in various countries around the world.

According to one of the biggest advocates of the "beware of deflation" scenario, Robert Prechter, we've been in a period of credit inflation rather than currency inflation.

This means our economy has seen a vast increase in debt — mortgages, credit cards, government spending and so on. At some point such bubbles reach a peak and implode, resulting in what I've been describing.

Prechter is predicting a crash that will make the Great Depression look like a walk in the park. Although we did see a partial crash in debt and in asset values from 2008 to 2009, it's not over yet.

It's important to understand, however, although deflation of the U.S. dollar will protect your purchasing power within the United States itself, there's no guarantee deflation will make the US dollar rise.

That's because the value of the US dollar is relative to other currencies. If the US suffers 5% deflation, for example, but deflation in the Eurozone is 10%, the US dollar will still slide against the euro.

Chapter 5

So What's It Going to Be — Inflation or Deflation?

Yes.

I don't know.

Both cases are credible. What's worse, according to deflation guru Robert Prechter, they're not even mutually exclusive. Hyperinflation could follow massive deflation.

Fortunately, I believe my 3 step plan protects you against both possibilities.

First, though let's consider the other major world currency players.

Chapter 6

Sizing Up the "Competition"

One big factor affecting the value of nation's currency is its national debt. Although many of us in the United States are upset about how much our government spends and owes, we're not the worst in the world.

According to CNBC, the United States is only Number 20 in the list of Top 20 debtor countries. This is calculating national debt as a percentage of Gross Domestic Product.

Of the 19 countries which owe more than we do, 17 are European, some in the EU, some not. Even Switzerland is included — the country known for its fiscal conservatism.

Another country is Australia. Hong Kong is also listed, although I'd simply count it as part of China.

After the US dollar, the next major world currency is the euro.

Is the Euro Up to the Job of Replacing the US Dollar?

The European Union consists of twenty-seven countries. Sixteen of them have adopted the euro as their currency: Austria, Belgium, Cyprus, Finland, France, Germany, Greece, Ireland, Italy, Luxembourg, Malta, the Netherlands, Portugal, Slovakia, Slovenia and Spain.

They're known as the Eurozone. The IMF says it's the world's second largest economy, behind the United States.

Monaco, San Marino, Andorra, Vatican City, Montenegro and Kosovo also use the euro. Many other countries, especially in Europe and Africa, peg their national currencies to the euro (as many national currencies are pegged to the US dollar).

Although the name "euro" was adopted in 1995, it was not until January 1, 2002 euro coins and notes went into circulation.

In October 2009 790 billion euros were in circulation, surpassing the US dollar. It's the world's second largest reserve currency.

Many want to see the euro replace the US dollar. It's certainly true since the euro's inception its value has risen from 82 cents to as much as $1.50, though as I write it's back to around $1.31.

However, all is not rosy in the Eurozone. Greece has been running a huge budget deficit even though EU rules forbid member countries from having budget deficits over 3% of GDP. Its ability to pay interest on its government bonds is in doubt.

In response to the crisis and to the demands from other EU countries for fiscal responsibility, the government of Greece has cut wages for government employees (20% of the workforce), raised taxes and frozen pensions.

However, in response the people of Greece rioted and protested for weeks.

And Greece is not the only Euro Zone country running a deficit, not even the largest. Portugal, Ireland, Italy and Spain may create problems in the near future.

What Greece is demonstrating is combining countries into one economic whole — despite vast differences in their local economies — is a lot easier said than done.

For one thing, the traditional government response to high budget deficits is to do exactly what the United States has been doing for years — allow inflation to devalue the currency.

However, Greece cannot do that. It's now stuck with the euro and the EU is stuck with Greece.

No less a currency expert than George Soros has said Germany must make concessions in response to the Greek crisis, or the euro and the EU itself were at risk.

However, as of late 2011, it does not appear European politicians are going to reach a credible agreement to save the current system.

Moreover, almost all European countries have welfare programs in place that seem absurdly generous to us Americans. Free healthcare, unemployment, disability pensions and pensions encouraging early retirement. That's not to mention many European workers are more highly paid than Americans thanks to pressure from labor unions. And get much more paid vacation time. The current president of France is known as a crazy right-winger because he thinks French workers should go back to working forty hours per week.

The recent worldwide recession is highlighting Greece now, but many other European countries are vulnerable.

And then there's the future...

Most European countries also have a large baby boomer population. They're now reaching retirement age. On the whole, their governments have expected less work out of them and have given them more money than is the case in the United States. Plus, in many European countries birth rates have fallen to below replacement values. This means there are fewer young workers supporting many more older workers.

They're facing the exact shortfall problem we are with Social Security and Medicare — only worse.

To supply cheap labor, most countries of Europe have admitted many immigrants from the Middle East and Africa. These people — largely Muslim — are not being assimilated into the cultures of their host countries, but they are having many more children than native Europeans.

If this demographic trend doesn't change, by the end of this century Europe will be largely Muslim.

Therefore, although many traders prefer the euro to the US dollar, it's got many long-term problems to overcome.

In the 1980s We Thought the Japanese Were Taking Over the World

The Japanese yen is the third major world currency, and the largest in Asia.

Japan was the first Asian country to modernize and develop an industrial base. Although it suffered massive damage during World War 2, with American help it rebuilt itself within one generation into an economic powerhouse.

During the 1980s it was seen as our economic rival. Japanese were buying up Hawaii and prime real estate throughout America. Its stock market index, the Nikkei, zoomed up, leaving the Dow behind in its dust.

Some naysayers pointed out Japanese real estate values were so high people were taking out condo loans lasting two generations and the earnings of Japanese companies didn't support their stratospheric stock prices. However, we were told, the Japanese system was different.

In 1989, however, the Nikkei crashed. Its high was 39,000. It's now — twenty years later! — around 8,900 (and in 2009 hit 7,000).

This is true despite the Japanese government lowering interest rates to nearly 0 and spending huge amounts of money on infrastructure.

Despite that, its per capita income is steadily dwindling.

A strong yen hasn't done the Japanese economy much good.

It could well be the yen is strong because the Japanese people have not been big spenders since the 1989 beginning of their prolonged recession.

Like many European countries, Japan's birth rate has fallen dramatically. If it doesn't reverse, Japan will be in a steep decline by the end of this century. Unlike Europe and the United States, they refuse to allow significant immigration.

In March 2011 northern Japan was hit by a incredibly powerful earthquake. This caused massive damage. So did the resulting tsunami.

And four nuclear power plants were damaged. I doubt the world yet knows – or will ever really know – how close they came to disaster or how much radiation was released.

This will be a long and costly clean-up for Japan.

Like the euro, the yen has many deep-rooted and difficult long-term problems.

Up to World War 2 the British Pound was the World's Supercurrency

Another major world currency is the Great Britain pound sterling.

At its peak, the British empire was the greatest in the history of the world and was an early leader in the Industrial revolution.

Although it's lost its power, Great Britain retains a lot of prestige and renown in the world. London is a major world financial center.

The pound is the third largest world reserve currency and the fourth most traded currency.

That said, the 2009 performance of the pound made the US dollar look good. It lost more ground to the euro and yen than we did.

Plus, Britain's economy is still stagnant, and unemployment is high. It also has a strong culture of entitlement.

Like the U.S., the U.K. runs a large trade deficit, and they're more dependent on imports than we are since they're a smaller country with fewer natural resources.

I'm sure the British will muddle through as they always do, but I don't see them growing their superpower status any time soon.

The Swiss Franc is the Most Admired

In many respects, the Swiss franc is a libertarian's dream. Switzerland is the world's longest running democracy. Because of their geographic position in the Alps, it's made sense for them to adopt a policy of strict neutrality in the politics of Europe, coupled with an extreme willingness and ability to defend their own territory.

"Don't mess with us and we won't mess with you" has been their political and military slogan for five hundred years.

Financially, the Swiss are most well-known for their banks and bank secrecy laws, including their former acceptance of numbered (anonymous) bank accounts. A lot of wealth from many places around the world is stored in Zurich. However, the United States has been able to obtain information on some US citizens with bank accounts in Swiss banks.

Prior to 2000, Swiss law required the franc to be backed 40% by gold. They changed the law, however, so the franc is no longer redeemable by gold.

The government of Switzerland still owns a lot of gold. It's no longer on a gold standard, but it still owns more gold for its currency than any other country.

The Swiss are some of the hardest working, most efficient workers. It is suffering from the economic downturn, projecting budget deficits into 2013. Their per capita income is among the highest in the world.

It maintains a positive balance of trade surplus. To maintain that, however, the Swiss National Bank will intervene to keep the franc from going too high in value over the euro and the US dollar, as they did recently in a massive way.

For a small country of only a few million people, Switzerland has an enormous impact on the rest of the world.

Australia is Rich in Natural Resources

Next up is the Australian dollar.

Australia is, in many ways I believe, like the United States. It's a freedom-loving country which unfortunately in recent years has allowed too much socialism and political correctness.

It does have a much lower population. From what I understand, although the continent is quite large, much of it is desert.

It is rich in natural resources, including gold and uranium, and therefore the increased demand for commodities has been boosting the value of its currency. Not only that, it's geographically close to Asia and so does a lot of trade with China, which buys Australian commodities.

Its dollar tends to rise and fall with the price of gold, so it's a way to benefit from owning gold without owning gold.

It's also benefiting from interest rates. In December 2009 The Reserve Bank of Australia raised rates to 3.75%, third rate hike in a row. This means investors seeking safe yields can earn much more on their money than in other developed countries.

Loony for the Loonie

Another currency play on natural resources is the Canadian dollar, often called the "loonie."

Canada contains a lot of natural resources from timber to oil to minerals that have yet to be fully developed. It does have fairly high unemployment (though below the United States) and low national interest rates.

Yet the loonie reached parity with the US dollar for the first time in decades.

To Sum Up

It's easy to diss the US dollar. It's not so easy to come up with an alternative.

Although the euro and yen get the media attention, both currencies have significant long-term problems. The British pound is going down faster than the US dollar.

The Australian and Canadian dollars both look good, but are dependent on energy and commodity demand. They could sink if the world enters a deflationary depression. The Swiss franc is probably the strongest of all, though Switzerland is not a major world power. Zurich however is a major financial center.

So let's look at the first "obvious" way to protect your US dollars — thinking you're smarter than everybody else in the world.

That is, trading on the foreign exchange markets.

Section Two

Specific Ways to Invest US Dollars to Protect Their Purchasing Power

Chapter 7

Trading on the Foreign Exchange Markets

This is perhaps the most obvious way people are trying to profit from the decline in value of the U.S. dollar.

At least, I'm assuming that's one reason for the incredible rise in recent years in the popularity of currency forex trading.

Personally, I find it appalling so many people are now promoting forex trading as a home business. You can find books with titles making it sound easy. You can spend hundreds or thousands of dollars for expensive courses and seminars. Not to mention software programs that guarantee they can make money trading for you. I've seen a video interview with one of the leaders in this niche online where he said he expects to make $30 million dollars. I wonder how many of his students will net anything close to that?

The Interbank Foreign Exchange Market is the Largest in the World — How Do You Think You Can Beat It?

Here's how it works.

The banks of the world are connected in an electronic network. To facilitate international commerce, they must constantly exchange currencies. It's called the interbank market. It's open from 5:15 PM Sunday night US Eastern Standard time (20:15 UTC) until 7:00 PM Friday night US Eastern Standard time (22:00 UTC).

When a manufacturer in Japan sells parts to an electronics company in Dubai, when an American tourist travels to Paris, when the President of Peru goes on a state visit to Australia... money changes hands. The currency of one country must be converted into the currency of another country.

Banks handle these transactions over the counter with each other. Nobody knows the precise volume since there's no central exchange, but best estimates are it runs around $3 trillion per day on the average and has reached as high as $6.5 trillion.

It's the largest and most liquid financial market in the world.

In business, it is legitimately used to hedge international transactions.

Let's say a U.S. corporation wants to buy a million widgets from a Japanese company. The American company wants to keep its costs down, and so has calculated it cannot afford to pay any more than $1 each for these widgets. Because it is an American company, it uses US dollars to price the widgets.

The Japanese company wants to make a profit by selling those widgets. At that volume, they can sell one million widgets for 120 yen each and be happy with their profit. Notice that, because they are based on Japan, they price the widgets in yen.

It just so happens that while they're negotiating this deal, one US dollar is worth 120 yen. Both companies are happy with that price, so they sign a contract for one million widgets for 120,000,000 yen — total.

Now let's say the Japanese company needs three months to manufacture and deliver those widgets. The U.S. corporation won't pay until after it receives them.

And neither company hedges this transaction.

If, at the end of those three months, upon completed delivery of the million widgets the US dollar is still worth 120 yen, there's no problem. The US company withdraws $1 million from its checking account and sends it to the Japanese company. Their bank converts that into 120,000,000 yen. Everybody's happy.

But that's extremely unlikely. In three months, the US dollar and yen will change in relative value. Maybe the US dollar will go up, maybe it will go down. Who knows? Nobody.

If at the end of those three months the US dollar is now trading at 125 yen, the American company now has to withdraw only $960,000 to come up with the 120 million yen required to pay for the widgets. They're happy.

However, the market could just as easily have gone the other way. If at the end of those three months the US dollar is now trading at 115 yen, then the U.S. company has to pay $1,043,478 for those widgets. That's $43,478 over their budget. They're not happy.

Therefore, modern corporations hedge the risk currency exchange rates will change. They give up the possibility of saving money in return for eliminating the risk of losing money.

The U.S. corporation will buy a foreign exchange contract enabling them to deliver 120 million yen in three months.

Until about 2000, the interbank market was available only to traders connected with major banks and corporations. Thanks to technological improvements, now small traders are also allowed to lose their money on it.

Can You Predict Short Term Shifts in Currency Values?

When you're trading currencies, you're betting on one currency against another.

(The US dollar doesn't go "up" or "down" in a vacuum. It goes up or down against another currency. It can go up against the euro even while it's going down against the yen.)

The most common pairs are EUR/USD and USD/JPY.

The top currency is the base currency. The bottom is always valued as one.

So if the euro is now worth 1.35 for one dollar, that's 1.35/1 = 1.35.

Another way of looking at this is — if you stayed in a 100 euro per night hotel in Berlin Germany it would cost you $135 per night.

Of course, in day to day forex trading the amounts are not rounded. The euro price is carried out to the fourth figure to the right of the decimal point.

Therefore, the euro is more likely to be worth 1.3571. The difference between that and 1.3572 is one pip.

Your goal as a trader is to see your position move as many pips as possible in the direction you desire.

The primary currencies traded are the US dollar (USD), the euro (EUR), the Japanese yen (JPY), the Swiss franc (CHD), the British pound (GBP), the Australian dollar (AUD) and the Canadian dollar (CAD).

It may be possible to trade other currencies, but unless you have some real good insider information regarding the Bangladeshi taka, why would you want to?

It's Now Simple and Easy for Small Traders to Get Started — Because the Sharks Want Your Money Too

You have to open an account with a forex broker. This may require a small or large amount of money. In a regular sized account, you trade full lots of currencies, which is $100,000. Thanks to leverage, you don't need to come up with that much, however. Some brokers will give you 1 to 100 leverage. That means you can trade a full $100,000 lot for only $1,000. If the trade goes your way, you can make a lot of money. Sound good? Remember some trades do not go your way, so you're quickly wiped out even if the market then turns around and goes as you predicted.

Some brokers allow mini-accounts. This means you can trade a total of $10,000 — again, using high amounts of leverage. The pips are $1.

Some online brokers now allow micro-accounts that trade a total of $1,000. The pips are only ten cents.

You'll probably have to pay extra for trading station software on your computer, plus a monthly charge. Plus an ongoing charge for a data feed.

Most forex brokers don't charge commissions. They make their money on the bid/ask spread.

You also need a strong understanding of everything that affects the relative value of currencies.

1. Interest rates.

The higher a country's interest rates, the more its money is worth. One reason for the US dollar's current decline is how the US Federal Reserve has lowered interest rates to almost zero.

2. Political actions.

Since at least Clinton's presidency, the US government has allowed the US dollar to weaken to make American made products more price-competitive in the world marketplace.

3. Economic facts.

The United States has run a balance of trade deficit for roughly fifty years, and it continues to grow alarmingly.

4. Weather and natural disasters.

5. Terrorist acts.

6. Inflation.

7. Central bank policies.

One reason for the euro's strength is European central banks have traditionally had a mandate to control inflation. Period.

In the United States, the Federal Reserve has acted to keep the economy moving. If that means lowering interest rates to encourage businesses to borrow money and hire more workers to reduce unemployment, then so be it.

8. Unforeseen events.

Not long ago the country of Greece came close to defaulting on its bonds, and the EU would not bail it out without it accepting a set of austerity conditions. Many Greeks rioted in the streets. Some experts began predicting the end of the euro.

Are they correct? I don't know.

What will happen next? I don't know, and neither do you.

Trading currencies on the foreign exchange market is not how to protect your purchasing power — unless you have the ability to predict the future with 100% accuracy.

Forex is the Largest Casino in the World

It's a form of gambling. You're competing with major banks, hedge funds, institutional traders, large and small corporations, and individual traders from around the world. They have a hundred times the computer power you do. They have hired Ph. Ds in Finance and Math. They run proprietary software. They have databases going back decades. Their computers make their trades automatically — as soon as they spot a possible winner they send in the order, while you're still scratching your head and examining the chart formation. And they often lose money too. What makes you think you can beat them?

Read the Blair Hull chapter of New Market Wizards by Jack Schwager. He was a successful currency trader because he traded for an institution and cultivated a wide network of contacts. They stayed in constant contact and passed along the latest news. Currency markets could change direction in a split second based on something a Japanese finance minister said.

I believe the markets are unpredictable.

Trading forex is a terrific way to lose purchasing power by throwing your US dollars away on books, courses and seminars. Then on trading platform software and data. Then on a sure-fire system or robot software programs. Then on brokerage commissions. And — last but not least — losing trades.

Yes, if you are financially able to stick with it for a while, you'll have some winning trades.

But as time goes by your expenses will exceed your income.

In the Long Run the US Dollar is Going Down Against Major Currencies, but Trading Uses Short Term Fluctuations and Volatility

I strongly advise you stay far away from forex trading — and anybody who wants to sell you on it.

Remember in today's world, currencies are simply commodities or products. They have a price.

You can be right on the long term trend – everybody knows that's down for the US dollar – but lose your shirt in the long run.

The current prices of dollars, euros, yen, francs, pounds and everything else depends on the constant ebb and flow of cash around the world.

Business transactions. Traders. Investors. Tourists. Family

transfers (for example, when Mexican workers living in the US use Western Union or Moneygram to send money to their wives in Mexico). Shoppers (when you buy a Rolls Royce you send dollars to Great Britain, strengthening the pound).

And it's constantly fluctuating. No matter how certain the world's experts are the US dollar is going downhill in the long term, in the next ten minutes it could strengthen enough to make you lose all your money.

The only way to stay in a trade for the long term is to put in the full $100,000 for a lot or $10,000 for a mini-lot. Then you can wait out short term fluctuations.

But if you have that kind of money, why would you go through all the hassle of opening an account, buy trading software, pay brokerage commissions and so on?

Chapter 8

What Has Actually "Beaten" Inflation Since 1975

I chose the beginning date of January 1, 1975 for various reasons.

At first I did so because one of the charts I needed started on that date, and it seemed a fair time, the middle of the worst economic decade since the 1930s. Then I learned that was the date Americans could again freely own gold coins and bullion, making it the perfect date.

I realize that misses a lot of the inflation and political disruption from the 1973 energy crisis, sugar and meat prices going up, Watergate and so on.

But the fact is, until then Americans could not legally own gold.

In 1971 President Nixon cut the official $35 per ounce connection between the US dollar and gold. Americans couldn't legally own gold, but everybody else in the Free World could, and until then could demand one ounce of gold from the US Treasury for every $35 of cash US dollars they turned in.

Anyway, by 1973 the world price of gold was floating according to supply and demand, so it started going up. However, Americans could not legally take part in that until President Ford signed Pub.L. 93-37 which went into effect January 1, 1975.

It's not possible to make 100% precise comparisons because in some cases the records end with the last full calendar month available. In other cases, I took the market price when I was writing this. But this analysis should still give an interesting look at the relative values.

And of course the precise numbers will have all changed by the time you actually read this. But they'll still effectively cover the last 36 years.

I wanted to compare Master Limited Partnerships, but they didn't exist back in 1975. I wanted to compare real estate home prices, but those indexes apparently don't go back to 1975 either.

Inflation

Let's start with measuring inflation. According to the federal government, it's the Consumer Price Index (CPI). Often it's the CPI for Urban Workers that is reported, but I'm using the CPI-W which is used for Social Security and many other COLA-based incomes.

Consumer Price Index (CPI)—the official inflation gauge

52.40 to 222.954 (end of May 2011)

Increase: 425.48%

(Source: Social Security Administration) http://www.ssa.gov/oact/STATS/cpiw.html

Let's see how well depending on government checks has stood up against inflation over the years.

However, Social Security recipients did not get a raise in 2010 or 2011. A 3.6% raise starts with 2012. Because SSA checks vary by individual, I'll use the Full Benefit Rate for individuals for Supplemental Security Income (SSI), to which the same COLAs were applied.

$146 to $674

Increase: 461.64%

(Source: Social Security Administration)
https://secure.ssa.gov/apps10/poms.nsf/lnx/0502001020

Therefore, based on official figures Social Security just about keeps up with the official rate of inflation, which makes sense given that's what the law mandates.

But of course, in a way we're really discussing the value of the US dollar, so let's examine that:

US dollar (as indexed against other major world currencies)

99 to 69.86 (as of May 2011)

Decrease: 29.44%

Which means, in effect, a 336.27% drop from 1975.

However, we have to be careful analyzing this figure, because it's not directly comparable to anything else.

99 / 29.44 = 336.27% decrease in dollar value since 1975 as compared to other world currencies.

Thus, shocking as it may seem, the US dollar has gone down less compared to other major world currencies than to domestic prices (the CPI), so perhaps it has more to fall against the euro, yen, etc.

(Source: St Louis Federal Reserve Bank)
http://research.stlouisfed.org/fred2/series/TWEXMMTH

Gold

$175 to $1,813 per ounce

Increase: 1,036%

(Source: Kitco)
http://www.kitco.com/scripts/hist_charts/yearly_graphs.plx

Gold's rise was relatively steady until the end of 1979 when Iranians took the staff of the American embassy hostage in November and in December the Soviet Union invaded Afghanistan. Then it zoomed from about $400 to a high of

$850. But a few months later, it dropped just as sharply back to around $400. Then it did a long slow slide to just over $251 in August 1999.

Nobody can deny it's gone up a lot since then. Now, its price increase has gone up over twice as much as inflation.

But I do have to point out I'm judging it as a very long term investment (35 1/2 years). For nearly twenty years, it was a total loser.

But then, that's what they tell us about buying and holding stocks. They go up in the long run, but can be losers for up to twenty years.

Silver

$4.30 to $38.72 per ounce

Increase: 900.46%

(Source: Trading Economics)
http://www.tradingeconomics.com/commodity/silver

Silver is another precious metal whose fate is often tied to gold. It too had an extreme price rise in 1979 (to over $48 per ounce), then an extreme drop in March 1980.

Some of its price rise may have reflected the world in crisis, but most of it was due to the Hunt Brothers attempting but failing to corner the world market.

So on one hand it's fair to say even today silver is below its record high. On the other, it's also fair to say that record price was artificial and is likely to remain the record high in real terms for a long time to come.

So silver's price increase is only slightly less than gold over this same period.

And, like gold, for about twenty years it was dead in the water.

What about that all important commodity, oil?

Crude Oil

$12.21 to $84.98 per barrel

Increase: 695.86%

At this point, gold's increase has outpaced that of oil. But oil has gone up nearly twice the official rate of inflation. But that's not a surprise because the official rate of inflation no longer includes energy costs.

(Source: Inflation Data)
http://www.inflationdata.com/inflation/inflation_rate/
historical_oil_prices_table.asp

How have stocks done?

Dow Jones Industrial Average

632 to 11,143

Increase: 1763.13%

(Source: Stockcharts
http://stockcharts.com/freecharts/historical/djia1900.html

S&P 500

68.65 to 1,172

Increase: 1,707.21%

(Source: S&P 500 charts
http://www.early-retirement-planning-insights.com/sp500-dividend-yields.html

and Econ Stats

http://www.econstats.com/eqty/eqem_mi_1.htm)

Thus, at this point, stocks overall have risen about four times as much as inflation, and nearly double gold and silver.

But it's fair to point out stocks have also had their ups and downs. In November 2007 when they reached their record high of 14,000 for the Dow, they would have looked even better.

But it's also true in the past 35 1/2 years stocks have been up more often than down.

What happens if we check out how well utility stocks and Real Estate Investment Trusts have done?

Utility Stocks

The Dow Jones Utility Index

80.27 to 413.09

Increase: 514.62%

(Source: Dow Jones Utility Index)

http://www.forecasts.org/data/data/djutilM.htm

Real Estate Investment Trusts

(equity only, because mortgage REITs are a different—and risky—kind of investment)

81.82 to 9,341.46

Increase: 11,417.08%

(Source: reit.com
http://www.reit.com/IndustryDataPerformance/
FTSENAREITUSRealEstateIndexHistoricalValuesReturns/
MonthlyIndexValuesReturns.aspx

Wow—REITs beat everybody, hands down. Of course, I can't promise you they'll do that in the next 35 years.

But now looking at these figures, I'm dissatisfied.

They're about asset prices. I'm an advocate of INCOME investing. What kind of income would a hypothetical January 2, 1975 investor have gotten for their money?

Well, to measure income from the US dollar, we're talking interest.

If somebody put $1,000 in a Treasury bond and kept rolling it over, how would they be doing?

Treasury Bonds (10 years, because Federal Reserve online data didn't go back to 1975 for 30 year bonds)

7.99 to 2.17

Decrease: 82.85%

Their income has gone down by 518.83%.

(Source: The Federal Reserve http://www.federalreserve.gov/releases/h15/data.htm

and

http://www.federalreserve.gov/releases/h15/update/default. htm

Gold

$0 to $0

Increase: 0%

Silver

$0 to $0

Increase: 0%

As an income investing advocate, I couldn't resist rubbing your face in these figures.

A bar of gold does not send out checks.

Neither does a bar of silver.

And actually I'm being nice, because gold and silver have costs of security, insurance and storage, so those numbers should be NEGATIVE. That is, owning gold and silver costs you money. But the precise amounts vary. And, besides, I'm not including brokerage commissions or taxes either.

And yes, I'm aware some gold and silver mining companies do send out dividend checks. If any such companies get into the one or more of the dividend-stock indexes I invest in, then I'll own them. I believe I do have a small piece of BHP Billiton in one of my ETFs.

Crude Oil

Barrels of oil also don't mail out checks.

Of course you can make money from them, if you can refine and process the oil, but that's pretty much like selling an asset, so it doesn't count.

S&P 500 Index

The S&P 500 started out January 2, 1975 (January 1 was a holiday of course) at 68.65. If someone invested $100 then, they received $4.99 in dividends for the year.

They've kept their original investment amount the same—$100.

We know that it now has a current market value of $1,707.21 (see above).

The current yield is 2.08%, so they are receiving a dividend check for:

1707.21 X 0.0208 = $35.51

35.51 / 4.99 = 711.62%

(Sources: Early Retirement http://www.early-retirement-planning-insights.com/sp500-dividend-yields.html and:

S&P 500 Dividend Yield)

http://www.multpl.com/s-p-500-dividend-yield/

Utility Stock Yields

12% to 4.0%

Again, let's say someone invested $100 in January 1975 in the stocks of the Dow Jones Utility Index.

The yield then was 12%, so they received $12 in dividends.

They kept that investment, which now has a market value of $413.09.

Its annual yield is now 0.04 X 413.09 = $16.52 is their current annual dividends.

Increase: 137.66%

(Sources: Seeking Alpha citing Dividends Don't Lie by Geraldine Weiss
http://seekingalpha.com/article/196989-fpl-group-undervalued-but-with-limited-upside-potential

and:

Financial News
http://www.financial8.com/financial_news/stock/IDU)

REITs

Again, we invested $100 in the index January 1975. That year's yield for equity REITs was 11.17 so we got $11.17 in income that year.

The market value of that $100 is now $9,341.46.

And that has a yield as of July 2011 of 3.43%, so our original $100 now pays:

9,341.46 X .0343 = $320.41

320.41 / 11.17 = 28,684.87%

(Source: Reit.com)
http://www.reit.com/IndustryDataPerformance/
FTSENAREITUSRealEstateIndexHistoricalValuesReturns/

MonthlyIndexValuesReturns.aspx

I do need to point out these income comparisons are NOT total return calculations. To do that, I'd have to get income figures for every year and market values for every year and use a spreadsheet or something to figure that out.

And then have to figure out brokerage commissions and taxes and I don't see the point.

However, I'm sure if we added in the 33 missing years of dividends, the total return of ordinary stocks, REITs and utilities would far exceed that of gold and silver.

Ordinary stocks, utility stocks and REITs pay out dividends every year, and those usually keep growing.

In the last 35 years, dividends from utility stocks didn't grow as much as inflation, but their market prices did.

Dividends from REITs far exceeded inflation.

Dividends from ordinary stocks also beat the official rate of inflation, as did their market prices as well.

Gold and silver prices have beat inflation.

Bonds—because their nominal values never change and interest rates have dropped dramatically—have utterly failed to keep up with inflation.

I guess that explains why my mother's friends who put their money into certificates of deposit griped to her so much about how much their income went down over the years.

I hope this helps everyone who is tempted by frightening headlines, radio ads and fear of inflation to buy gold to think long and hard before they do so.

The US dollar has lost a lot of purchasing power since 1975.

In April 1980, the month gold dropped back down to $450 per ounce, the government Consumer Price Index was 81.

As of March 2010 it was 217.

To match its 1980 peak of $850, gold would now have to be $2,277.

To be fairer, let's forget that short run up to $850 and use gold at $450 per ounce. That's $1,205.

Gold is now around $1,813 per ounce.

Congratulations. If you'd bought gold at $450 per ounce in 1980 and held on to it, it'd now be worth just one and a half as much as if you'd stuffed the cash into your mattress.

And it's worth that much now only after an extreme nine year run up. For over twenty years your gold was worth much less than what you paid for it.

And even less in term of purchasing power.

The Dow Jones Industrial Average was around 800 then. If you'd put that $450 into the stock market it'd now be $6,187 if you didn't reinvest dividends.

If you reinvested dividends, you'd have a lot more money than that.

If you simply put your $450 into a money market account and reinvested the interest, you'd have pretty much kept up with inflation, though not have exceeded it.

And you also would have had the ability to spend $100+ on bills when you needed to — unlike with gold.

Ah, but isn't gold a great thing to have in dangerous, insecure times?

When gold was universally recognized as money, I'm sure it was easier to find food and shelter with gold coins than with nothing. I'm also sure when wealthy families had to flee their city to escape barbarians or a revolution, they packed gold coins and jewelry rather than their dining room table and chandelier, no matter how expensive those were.

(In 1986 when Ferdinand Marcos was deposed as president of The Philippines, he and his wife Imelda took jewelry but not her thousands of pairs of shoes.)

I'm also sure gold-backed warehouse receipts issued in Venice didn't mean much in Paris.

We've also seen how the Soviet invasion of Afghanistan pushed the price of gold from $450 to $850.

But it fell back to $450 in a few months.

And drifted down until reaching a low of $251 in August 1999.

Now, I have to admit if we did the same analysis as above, but started in August 1999, the results would look a lot different.

In those nearly 12 years gold has gone from $251 to $1,813 – up 722.31%.

At that time, the Dow Jones Average was just below where it is now at 11,400 (it reached its current level just a few months later.)

Therefore, the Dow has gone up almost nothing in that same period.

Chapter 9

The Traditional "Stores of Value" — Gold (and Silver)

As soon as the subject of protecting yourself against inflation or other financial crises comes up, the first thing many people think of is gold.

(And silver, but for simplicity, except for when I discuss silver specifically, I'll just discuss gold.)

We've seen it works – sometimes, given a long enough period, but not as well as many alternatives.

The local conservative talk radio station in St. Louis plays a lot of commercials for gold dealers. Various national conservative talk show hosts have been promoting specific gold services for years.

Several local hosts who give financial advice are bombarded every week with the question, "Should I buy gold?" They joke about it on the air.

Remember how in Chapter One we discussed how money has

grown from being of actual value in itself (beaver pelts or dried rice) to being a representation of value (warehouse receipt and gold certificates) to being purely symbolic (fiat money) representing social and political trust?

Yes, I know gold has been used as money for thousands of years. As a symbol of wealth its origins are lost in prehistory. It's an integral part of our myths, legends and figures of speech.

But what is the actual, objective intrinsic value of gold?

It's bright. It's shiny. It's beautiful. It conducts electricity well.

If you've ever gone into a Bangkok jewelry store with a massive inventory of gold necklaces on display, you know it's dazzling.

It can be made into many beautiful objects. 80% of it is made into beautiful jewelry women (and many men) love to wear. And when you do wear genuine gold jewelry, it doesn't turn your skin green.

Gold in the form of jewelry is still treated as wealth by many people around the world. Many poor families in Asia keep their wealth in the form of the wife's jewelry. When they have an extra expense, she takes a bracelet to the local pawnshop. That's better than a checking account.

It's durable. Retrieve a bar of gold from a Spanish galleon sunk in 1693 and it's still bright, shiny and beautiful.

It's even useful. I have a tiny amount of it in a crown over one of my teeth. It conducts electricity better than copper so it's valuable for many electronic processes.

But does any of that justify the international obsession with this metal?

Does the United States keep tons of gold at Fort Knox because jewelry and tooth fillings are such a high national priority?

Many Investing Experts Advise You Not to Get Emotional About Your Investments, but Gold is Hyper-Emotional

I absolutely sympathize with the "hard money" crowd who advocate tying the value of our currency to something with enduring value, to eliminate the constant inflation we now experience with fiat money.

However, I have to tell you this story. I read it in the book How to Make $1,000,000 in the Stock Market Automatically by Robert Lichello.

I wish I could recommend the entire book to you. Unfortunately, it's difficult to follow his advice without an accurate crystal ball, so I can't.

However, I do recommend his outlook on gold. I have to give great credit to this story, because it helped shape my investing philosophy.

Mr. Lichello was a Marine posted in Japan during the aftermath of World War 2. The country had been thoroughly bombed. It was devastated, in ruins.

Mr. Lichello needed to raise some money, so he went to a local gold dealer and tried to sell the man his gold watch.

The man shook his head. No.

But it's real gold, Lichello assured him.

The man waved his hand at his store. The shelves were full of gold jewelry, gold figures, plates and so on.

"Everybody wants to sell gold," he told Lichello. "Nobody wants to buy."

That's instructive right there, but it's not the end of the story.

Lichello still needed to raise some cash. He had a buddy who always seemed to have plenty of spending money, so he approached his friend for advice.

"Just follow me," his friend said.

First stop: their PX. The friend sweet talks the Japanese lady at the counter into giving him twice his allowed ration of cigarettes, soap and chocolate.

Then he takes these to a Japanese black market dealer, who gladly pays for them with a big wad of Japanese currency.

When push comes to shove, people prefer necessities over a bright and shiny metal — no matter how beautiful it is.

As I related in a previous chapter, around 1870 in the United States new silver mines created so much inflation we had to go to a pure gold standard, which created highly unpopular deflation.

But — really! — what sense does that make?

Prospectors found some good areas of ground holding a lot of brightly shiny metal that's good for jewelry and teeth fillings. Investors supplied capital to buy mining equipment. Managers hired laborers and together they brought up and refined a lot of that bright, shiny beautiful metal.

Just what did that have to do with the price of eggs in New York City? Or the price of wheat in Chicago?

Except for making lots of new jewelry and, perhaps, supplying material for teeth fillings and electrical devices, what overall real value did that silver bring to the national economy?

Very little.

On the Gold Standard, Gold Mining Causes Inflation

Same with gold. Gold mining companies find, mine and refine gold. If we were on a gold standard, we'd then have more gold to go into circulation. Just how would that create new and additional wealth?

Does that bright, shiny metal feed any hungry children? Does it cure the sick? Does it put a roof over your head? Or even entertain you?

No. So how — exactly — is the economy better off with additional gold coins in circulation?

It seems to me finding new sources of gold and putting it into the economy in the form of monetary coins — without an equivalent increase in goods and services available — is just another form of inflation.

And when British frigates sank Spanish galleons loaded with New World gold, that was a form of deflation, because that gold was then unavailable to be used as money.

Perhaps I could even argue the discovery of the New World itself is an example against gold and silver.

Spain was the initial beneficiary of the discovery of America, and did become rich through stealing gold from the Native Americans. However, they lost their advantage to France and England.

France sent trappers and trades people who bought animal skins from the Native Americans, then sent them to Europe for fashionable clothing.

England sent over colonists who grew cotton and tobacco. Although England eventually lost control over its colonies, it reaped a much longer and richer harvest by focusing on products people in Europe wanted to buy.

Spain took the short-cut of taking the "store of value" — gold — and treating it as real wealth. Yes, Spain was able to buy many more things, but when the gold ran out it ceded world power leadership to England. (And it continued on as a secondary world power by draining real goods from its colonies in Latin American and The Philippines.)

England increased its wealth by using land and labor to create value. (Yes, they stole the labor of slaves, and that's wrong, but they didn't direct it toward a bright shiny yellow metal, but in-demand agricultural products.)

Therefore, although I do sympathize with people who want to tie money to actual value (goods and services that meet human needs and desires), I don't understand their argument gold and silver does this. I don't grasp the logical connection.

But isn't gold a safe haven from economic problems, especially inflation?

That's the common story.

Sometimes it's true, but sometimes it isn't.

The 1970s Were a Scary Decade

During the 1970s, inflation in the United States ran incredibly high. If you're more than ten years younger than I am, you can't understand the constant stress of going to a store and not knowing how much food you could buy — because this week's prices would be higher than last week's, but you couldn't know by how much.

If prices remained the same — this used to happen with candy bars — the product was smaller, so you got less for your money.

By January 1980, the price of gold hit a 20th century peak of $850 per ounce.

Protecting its owners from inflation and world uncertainty, right?

Not quite. In November 1979 the price was around $450. The extreme run-up happened within just a few months, and seems to have been sparked by the Soviet invasion of Afghanistan in December 1979.

No Safe Haven From Nuclear Winter

Gold rapidly spiked to $850, then just as quickly — by April 1980 — was back down to around $450 per ounce.

What happened? Nobody knows exactly. Inflation was still high and would remain so until 1982. Soviet troops still occupied Afghanistan — and would remain there many years.

The US embassy employees were still hostages in Iran, and would remain there until president-elect Ronald Reagan's swearing in ceremony in January 1981.

Yet gold continued to drift down. Sure, it had ups as well as downs, but it had more downs. By August 1999 it was only $251 per ounce.

Does that mean we had no inflation from 1980 to 1999?

Hardly. As I mentioned, inflation remained severe through 1982. After that, the rate of inflation did gradually taper down, but it was certainly significant.

The 1980s and 1990s Were Also Scary Decades

As I noted above, that's not because the Soviet Army withdrew from Afghanistan. It would remain there another nine years or so.

It's not because inflation was conquered. It remained high for two more years. It's gone down since then, but took twenty-five years to do so.

Is it because the world suddenly became a peaceful, secure-seeming boring place?

Not hardly. The early 1980s were full of tension between the United States and the Soviet Union. President Reagan's decision to place cruise missiles and Pershing II missiles close to the U.S.S.R. greatly increased people's fear of nuclear war, sparking huge protests in Europe and many in the United States.

There was great public debate and fear of a even a small nuclear war destroying us with a "nuclear winter."

The Sandinistas were in charge of Nicaragua while we engaged in a small scale contra war against them. Marxists guerillas were active in El Salvador and Guatemala.

In 1989 the Chinese government crushed the Tienanmen Square protests. The Berlin Wall fell.

In August 1990 Saddam Hussein invaded Kuwait, triggering

the first Gulf War.

The Soviet Union broke up. This was good news, but created massive uncertainty about what would follow.

And this uncertainty was made serious by the breakup of Yugoslavia and the Bosnian war.

In the late 1990s the United States government went through extreme political turmoil over the issue of impeaching President Clinton.

Those two decades were anything but quiet and peaceful, secure and boring.

The price of gold, however, was boring.

Do you really wish to stake your financial future on a metal which, in modern times, has shown such poor performance?

You may object the price has been kept artificially law through central bank selling, and that's a fair observation.

I'd have say first central banks are part of the market and have just as much right to sell gold when and for whatever reason as anybody else, so the market price is never "artificial."

I agree central banks have kept the price down for political reasons.

That gold is such a political football is yet another reason not to depend on it.

If gold's price goes too high and President Obama decides he doesn't want Americans to own it, so he sells the contents of Fort Knox to force the price down — who's going to stop him? You?

Also, although gold and silver probably will continue to go up in price because of US dollar inflation (I admit that), inflation is only half my fear.

If the economy crashes because of deflation, the price of gold and silver will go down with other assets.

Therefore, although gold is a possible hedge against inflation, it won't protection you from a deflationary depression.

Where You Keep Your Gold Is Also a Risky Decision

Another hassle with gold as a "safe haven" is the decision where to keep it.

That must be based on how bad you expect things to get.

If you believe the US dollar will continue to drift lower and gold will remain an in-demand hedge, but the world financial markets will continue to function — then you'll want to invest in gold's exchange traded fund, gold mutual funds, or in a professional storage vault or gold mining stocks.

If you believe there'll be a world market financial collapse, you want your gold is a local safe deposit box or storage vault.

If you believe the US government will come after your gold (as it did during the Great Depression), you must keep it in your safe at home.

If you believe there'll be a total breakdown of civilization, you'll need enough guns to guard your gold. And, just as in post-war Japan, it may not be as popular as you now believe it will, because it's not edible.

Yet the World Continues to Value Gold

However, I'm not going to tell you not to invest in some gold. I believe it's an important hedge against financial catastrophe.

Although I see only its value for jewelry, electronics and teeth, much of the world disagrees with me. Many central banks around the world continue to hoard their gold, including Fort Knox.

Millions of investors continue to buy it. One gold expert I read speculated Sovereign Wealth Funds (investments funds set up by governments outside of their usual monetary reserves) are buying up gold ETFs.

So long as much of the world sees gold and silver as stores of value, they are. Who am I to argue with that?

Therefore, a well-diversified disaster preparation portfolio must include some.

Maybe the price of gold will soon be $10,000 per ounce, so let's see how to take advantage of that — just in case.

Chapter 9-A

Gold Bars

If you have the money, you can buy bars of gold. Find a trustworthy dealer.

I have two big problems with this strategy.

One is you must pay storage fees. You lose some purchasing power just by keeping your gold secure. One service I checked out has fees of 0.00375% of the ask price every six months, with a $15 minimum.

You could keep it in your home, but one night you may make a thief very happy.

My second problem is you can't sell pieces of large bars. What if you have a five-ounce bar of gold but need to sell only half an ounce? You have to sell the entire bar.

This could also be a problem in the event of a total economic collapse. You may not want to trade a large chunk of gold for three loaves of bread.

And if your bars are stored in a secure place, how will you gain access to them?

Unless you happen to live near a gold storage warehouse, your gold will be in a distant city. What if you can't get there? What if you get there but it's closed? – perhaps already looted, or raided by the government.

Chapter 9-B

Pieces of Eight

One easy way to own gold is simply to buy gold coins.

South African Krugerrands, American Gold Eagles, Canadian Gold Maples, Chinese Gold Pandas, and Australian Nuggets are exactly one ounce. From my research, Krugerrands have the lowest premiums. Therefore, they're the best bargain.

If the price goes up as much as people hope, these coins would be too large for normal everyday shopping.

So you should also keep small denominations on hand.

Make sure you do not buy gold coins that have numismatic value. That is, value as a collectible coin. This includes not only very old and rare coins, but newly issued coins and proof sets.

Buying such coins is an investment in a hobby, not in gold. You're paying far more than the value of the gold in the coin. If all you want is the gold, you're overpaying.

To turn them into cash depends on the existence of a market of coin collectors. During an economic catastrophe that market may not exist. Selling them for their gold value alone could be your only choice, but could make you take a loss or not gain as high a profit as you desire.

Find a local dealer, buy what you want and put them away in a safe place until you need them.

But it's a lot easier to let someone else store the gold for you, so you can spend it online.

Chapter 9-C

Digital Gold Currency

One major complaint I have with owning physical gold is, like owning stocks that don't pay dividends, you can't profit from your ownership without selling it. And that's a hassle.

Thanks to the Internet, it's now possible to use your gold to buy things online using the digital equivalent of gold warehouse receipts.

In the future that may be accessible via debit cards, but apparently no such system yet exists.

The digital gold currency company owns and securely stores a quantity of gold (or silver, platinum or palladium, but gold is no doubt most popular).

You open an account and transfer some of your currency to them. The equivalent amount of their gold then becomes yours. The value of your account will fluctuate with the market price of the metal. You do pay a storage fee.

You can transfer gold to other account holders, including using it to pay for products and services.

As I recall, the original idea was to facilitate anonymous financial transactions.

However, the government now requires them to verify the identity of customers.

e-Gold was the First Digital Gold Currency

The first big name in this field was e-gold, using the company name e-gold Ltd. operated by Gold & Silver Reserve Inc. in 1996. e-gold Ltd. is incorporated in Nevis, Lesser Antilles and it was operated out of Florida.

In 2007 the United States Department of Justice indicted the owners on four counts of violating money laundering regulations. They plead guilty in July 2008.

While not necessarily intended by the company, some e-gold account holders have used the system to commit various crimes online.

Although still operating, e-gold is no longer accepting new accounts, and old accounts are dwindling.

Other digital gold providers have been associated with fraud. After all, it's easier to say you have gold in storage than to actually incur the expense of buying and storing it. In the old days, everybody in town would have known Joe the goldsmith had a locked store room with gold on its shelves. You could see that for yourself just by dropping in and chatting with Joe. However, online you're trusting people you don't know who live far away from you.

I recommend you not do business with any digital gold provider that does not allow regular third-party audits.

I'm dubious about the need for digital gold currency, especially for Americans who have access to credit cards, bank debit cards, Paypal accounts and other online payment processors. It may be useful for people who live in countries where the financial infrastructure is less developed, especially in countries where Paypal is not fully operating.

They are a convenient way to buy, store and actually use gold. But it seems to me the main benefit is the "romance" of using gold to pay for an ebook or a sweater.

If the US dollar becomes nearly worthless to the rest of the world, will you really be ordering much from online catalogs? I guess if you own enough gold, you still could.

However, at your local supermarket you'd want some gold coins or a gold debit card (which doesn't yet exist, at least not in widely recognized form).

Yet these gold-based transactions are not reversible. That's one reason they're attractive to scammers. If you buy something on eBay and never receive it, you're stuck.

The One Digital Gold Currency Company Everybody Recommends

I'm not risking my own reputation by recommending them, but if I were going to use a digital gold currency company, it'd be GoldMoney.

GoldMoney is the only government registered and financially regulated digital gold currency company. They have quarterly audits every three months by a Big Four accounting firm.

They're based on Jersey, British Channel Islands, which is a British crown dependency in the English Channel. That's where their web servers are located.

But their precious metals is in vaults in London, Zurich and Hong Kong.

You can easily open an account with them and buy gold, silver and platinum. You can let them keep it in storage or take physical possession of it yourself — up to a 400 oz gold bar.

If you keep the value in your account, you can switch between gold, silver and platinum — though this is a form of trading or speculation and you'll probably lose money unless you can foresee the future.

You can keep some of your GoldMoney account in a major currency, and most customers are allowed to switch back and forth between US dollars, yen, euros, Swiss francs and so on.

However, American customers are not allowed to do this. Therefore, for us, a GoldMoney account is not a way to hedge our US dollars using other currencies.

They have their own patented gold money system — goldgrams. This is what you can use to pay for goods online. One goldgram equals the monetary value of one gram of gold.

In my own online buying, I have not noticed any merchants who accept digital gold currency as a form of payment, but this could change.

If you are in business and outsource a service to someone in another country, sending them goldgrams may be a convenient way to pay them.

If you really want to own physical gold, this is good way to do so and yet still have convenient use of your money.

GoldMoney is also approved for U.S. self-directed Individual Retirement Accounts. See The Entrust Group if this appeals to you.

Chapter 9-D

Gold and Silver Exchange Traded Funds

One simple way to profit from the rising price of gold, without the risk of owning actual metal coins or bullion, is through Exchange Traded Funds (ETF). They either hold gold themselves, or use derivatives to track the price of gold.

ETFs offer investors a way to profit from the rise of gold without taking possession of any of the metal or worrying about whether a particular mine will pan out or not.

In the United States, the gold ETF is

SPDR Gold Trust (formerly streetTRACKS Gold Shares) **(NYSE Arca: GLD)**

GLD buys and sell gold bullion. Each share is about one-tenth the price of an ounce of gold. The bullion is kept in the form of London Good Delivery bars (400 oz.) and held in an allocated account. The Custodian is HSBC Bank USA, in its London vault.

GLD was first listed on the exchange in November 2004. Shares also trade in Singapore, Hong Kong, and Tokyo. It owns over 1,000 tonnes.

The expense ratio is 0.40%.

Because it owns a physical metal, GLD earns no income and pays no dividend. However, because of the expense of storing it, taxpayers are allowed to include those expenses on their tax returns. It includes a lot of calculations that aren't user-friendly.

iShares COMEX Gold Trust (IAU) began January 21, 2005.

It too seeks to track the market price of gold, minus fund expenses. (The expense ratio is 0.25%.)

ETFS Gold Trust ETF or Physical Swiss Gold Shares (Public, NYSE:SGOL) is yet another one, begun September 9, 2009. Expense ratio is 0.39%.

PowerShares DB Gold Fund (NYSE Arca: DGL) uses future contracts to replicate the performance of gold. It does not own the physical metal.

Therefore its expense ratio is 0.52%.

You can find longer lists of gold ETFs, but they include Exchange Traded Notes (ETNs) which do not own gold but are debts of the issuing company. This means if the ETN issuer goes out of business you lose your investment. They also include ETFs using leverage (doubling how much you lose when gold's price falls) and ETFs listed on exchanges outside the U.S.

Because IAU and GLD have the same expense ratio, they're

equivalent, and superior to the more expensive SGOL and DGL. All you need is one.

Silver ETFs

Because silver has many industrial uses, its price also fluctuates with economic events in those industries. That is, with supply and demand.

On April 21, 2006 iShares launched its **Silver Trust (NYSE:SLV)** Exchange Traded Fund. The fund owns a reserve of silver. If you buy shares of this ETF, you have ownership interest in those reserves — all 304,000,000 of them. It has over nine thousand tonnes of silver in trust.

The fund's expense ratio is 0.5%. It too pays no dividends.

There's also the **ETFS Physical Silver Shares ETF (NYSE: SIVR)**. Its expense ratio is 0.30%.

PowerShares DB Silver Fund (NYSE: DBS). It does not hold metal silver. It uses futures contracts to replicate the market price of silver. Management expense ratio is 0.75%.

You can find lists of other silver ETFs. However, they're either Exchange Traded Notes that introduce the credit risk of the issuing company, use leverage or are listed on exchanges outside the U.S.

SIVR would be my choice because its expense ratio is lower than SLV's.

As with all ETFs, however, you must pay a commission every

time you have your broker buy ETF shares. This is fine if you have one large lump sum of cash to invest. If you're making frequent purchases (such as using deductions from your paycheck), this gets expensive.

If you're in that situation, you must consider mutual funds. I dislike them for reasons explained at length in Income Investing Secrets.

Yet I must admit small investors making regular investments cannot afford to pay commissions.

However, there's a problem. Mutual funds don't have the same structure as ETFs. They can't just buy up a lot of gold or silver and sell you ownership shares in it. Nor can they use futures contracts to replicate gold and silver market prices.

They have to own stocks or bonds.

Of course, there are many that do own stocks and bonds in gold and silver companies, but that's not the same as investing to replicate the price of gold or silver.

Therefore, first we'll talk about companies engaged in the business of gold or silver.

Chapter 9-E

Precious Metals Mining Companies

One common way of investing in gold, silver and other precious metals is to buy shares of mining stocks.

I can understand this to the degree mining companies pay dividends. Some of the major ones do, though most of the smaller ones do not.

However, you must also remember you're adding the business risk of the company on top of the risk of the price of gold. A poorly run gold mining company can lose money even while the price of the metal shoots up.

Plus, you're exposed to the fluctuations in production costs. When the price of oil goes up, so does the cost of using energy to mine and refine gold. Mines located in emerging countries are subject to political risk.

The three top companies are Barrick, Newmont and Placer Dome.

Below them are a number of other large, well-run and established companies. Then there are many more not so large, extremely speculative junior mining stocks.

If a company owns only a few mines, those could run out of gold and put the company out of business despite the price of gold. Some junior mining stocks never even find gold to mine.

This situation calls for an important strategy to minimize risk — diversification.

If you must invest in precious metals mining company, use Exchange Traded Funds if you have one large sum of money. If you invest small amounts on a frequent basis, reconsider your priorities. Gold mining stocks should not be your initial method of protecting your US dollars. They're too risky.

Gold Mining ETFs

The **Market Vectors Gold Miners ETF (NYSE Arca: GDX)** tracks the Amex Gold Miners Index. It also includes silver and platinum mining as well as gold, and that's good. It's additional diversification. Its expense ratio is 0.53%. Dividend is currently $0.11 per share.

The **Market Vectors Junior Gold Miners ETF (GDXJ)** seeks to replicate the Market Vectors Junior Gold Miners Index. It owns fifty-five stocks and has an expense ratio of 0.54%. It started in November 2009. There's no dividend. The description reveals some of the companies haven't even started operations yet. This, therefore, is essentially a gamble.

PowerSharesGlobalGoldandPreciousMetalsPortfolio

(PSAU) tracks the NASDAQ OMX Gold and Precious Metals Index. The expense ratio is 0.75%. It does not pay a dividend.

Out of the three:

GDXJ is far too speculative.

PSAU does not pay a dividend and has the highest expense ratio.

GDX pays a dividend and has the lowest expense ratio. That makes GDX the clear winner.

Gold Mining Mutual Funds

There are a lot of them.

I personally don't like mutual funds, but I do have to recognize for people who make regular small contributions they're more cost effective than exchange traded funds.

(Actually, DRIPs are best for such investors, but they aren't available for ETFs, though some brokerages do allow automatic reinvestment of dividends of ETFs.)

First on the list of where I'd invest (assuming I wished to invest in precious metals mining companies) is Vanguard Precious Metals and Mining Fund (VGPMX). The expense ratio is 0.27%. Dividends are currently $0.053 per share.

Van Eck International Investors Gold A (INIVX). Expenses 1.25%. Annual dividends $0.679.

U.S. Global Investors World Precious Minerals

(UNWPX). Expenses 1.85%. Annual dividends $2.97.

U.S. Global Investors Gold and Precious Metals (USERX). Expenses 1.82%. Annual dividends $0.

USAA Precious Metals and Minerals (USAGX). Expenses 1.15%. Annual dividends $0.62.

Tocqueville Gold (TGLDX). Expenses 1.34%. Dividends $0.

Rydex Precious Metals Inv (RYPMX). Expenses 1.28%. Annual dividends $0.03 (first in six years and none since November 2010).

ProFunds Short Precious Metals Inv (SPPIX). Expenses 1.88%. No dividends since 2008.

ProFunds Precious Metals UltraSector Inv (PMPIX). Expenses 1.61%. No dividends since 2008.

Oppenheimer Gold & Special Minerals C (OGMCX). Expenses 1.88%. Annual dividends $1..

Oppenheimer Gold & Special Minerals B (OGMBX). Expenses 1.98%. Annual dividends $4.16.

Oppenheimer Gold & Special Minerals A (OPGSX). Expenses 1.06%. Annual dividends $4.44.

OCM Gold Investor (OCMGX). Expenses 1.93%. No dividends.

Midas (MIDSX). Expenses 2.10%. Dividend: $6.22.

Prudential Jennison Natural Resources C (PNRCX).
Expenses 1.90%. Annual dividends $0.51.

Prudential Jennison Natural Resources B (PRGNX).
Expenses 1.90%. Annual dividends $0.57.

Prudential Jennison Natural Resources A (PGNAX).
Expenses 1.20%. Annual dividends $0.57.

AIM Gold & Precious Metals Inv (FGLDX). Expenses
1.35%. Annual dividends $0.33.

ING Global Natural Resources A (LEXMX). Expenses
1.53%. No current dividends.

GAMCO Gold AAA (GOLDX). Expenses 1.44%. Annual
dividends $1.33.

Franklin Gold and Precious Metals C (FRGOX). Expenses
1.70%. Annual dividends $0.

Franklin Gold and Precious Metals A (FKRCX).
Expenses 0.95%. Annual dividends $0.

First Eagle Gold C (FEGOX). Expenses 1.97%. Annual
dividends $0.56.

First Eagle Gold A (SGGDX). Expenses 1.22%. Annual
dividends $0.73.

Fidelity Select Gold (FSAGX). Expenses 0.91%. Dividends
$0.

Evergreen Precious Metals C (EKWCX). Expenses 1.85%. Dividends: 0.10.

Evergreen Precious Metals B (EKWBX). Expenses 1.85%. Dividends: 0.06.

Evergreen Precious Metals A (EKWAX). Expenses 1.10%. Dividends: 0.

DWS Gold & Precious Metals S (SCGDX). Expenses 1.15%. Annual dividends $1.47.

RiverSource Precious Metals & Mining A (INPMX). Expenses 1.00%. Annual dividends $0.

American Century Global Gold Investment (BGEIX). Expenses 0.69%. Annual dividends $0.

Chapter 9-F

Gold Doesn't Write Checks, Isn't Always a Safe Harbor, and Isn't Even Edible

I've made it clear I consider gold more trouble and risk than it's worth.

I may be proven wrong.

I don't know the future. But I also believe the many gold bugs promoting gold aren't psychic either.

To me, the most sensible thing is to invest a small percentage of your portfolio in gold — just in case.

But only do so if you have a large portfolio of other investments. If you're just getting started, gold — especially mining stocks — is not for you.

I admit, one reason I object to gold is metal doesn't write checks. It does not pay dividends. And to own substantial amounts safely you have to pay someone to store it. That costs money and will be inconvenient if we ever have a true economic emergency.

Investing in Anything for Capital Gains is a Trap

This means gold is a capital gains asset, like shares of Cisco stock. Its price will go up and down. But no matter how high it goes, you cannot benefit from it without selling it.

Selling it at a profit means capital gains taxes. Selling at any price means paying a commission.

Selling at any price means losing out on future price appreciation.

Failing to sell can mean losing your opportunity to realize profits — perhaps for twenty-five years.

If you'd owned gold in January 1980 do you think you would have sold it for $850 per ounce? Many people did not, because the doomsayers and Chicken Littles were predicting it'd go to $2,000.

Would you have held on to it for over twenty years, waiting for it to go back up?

Now that it's over $800 again, did you sell to break even (after twenty-five years) or are you still waiting for it to reach $2,000?

Once it does – and it's getting close – will you sell or wait for it to reach $5,000 as some experts predict it will?

If you'd bought gold in 1975 for $160 per ounce at what point would you have sold it? Would you have waited for it to reach

$850 per ounce, or would you have been out long before that?

Most painfully...what would you have done if you'd bought it at that $850 peak? Many people did, you know.

How would you feel if you buy gold at its peak, lose over 40% of your investment within 3 months, and then watch it slide even further for TWENTY YEARS?

Investing for capital gains sets up that vicious emotional tug of war between fear and greed. Take profits now or wait until they're bigger? But what if they don't grow any bigger? What if the peak is in the past?

And with gold, these emotions are magnified. They can distort your thinking, because to profit big-time, you're hoping for catastrophe. On one level of your mind, you're a nice person who doesn't want to see people hurt by an economic earthquake. Yet the selfish part of you that wants to make a profit, is hoping to be proven right.

Of course, you're not personally responsible for either outcome.

And the worst thing is, as I wrote in the first section of this chapter, you can be right and still be wrong.

That is, you can buy gold, see the dollar collapse and yet your gold investment doesn't act as the "safe haven" everybody says it does.

It was a terrible investment throughout the 1980s and 1990s and those were decades of great political, economic and military turmoil.

In fall 1997 and summer 1998 when the currencies of many Southeast Asian countries (and Korea) dropped like a rock and Russia's stock market lots 90% of its nominal value, people in emerging countries around the world sold their gold and invested in a "safe haven" called the US dollar.

They drove US Treasuries through the roof. I remember it well, because I lost thousands of dollars in an option trade.

But the Principle of Diversification Suggests You Should Have Some Gold, So You're Prepared in Case It Does Go Up When the Dollar Falls

Have a few gold bars or coins in a safe in your house, in case of total economic and systemic collapse. (Though if that happens guns, stored food and water, and first aid supplies will probably do you more good.)

Own some gold through GoldMoney, so if the dollar collapses you can sell your ownership in that gold for enough money to live on.

Own shares of the GLD or IAU ETFs — just in case the market price of gold skyrockets.

However, don't place any more than 5% of your portfolio into gold and silver.

If you have so much money you can afford to speculate/gamble/play, then buy some shares of GDX. Although it does pay dividends, they aren't high or dependable enough for income investors such as myself.

If a gold/silver/precious metals company does have a superior record of paying dividends, it will be included in a Mergent Dividend Achievers index and I'll wind up owning it that way.

If precious metals can't protect us, maybe ordinary commodities can.

Chapter 10

Commodities

Commodities is a broad term that covers basic material goods.

Wheat. Corn. Iron. Copper. Timber. Orange juice. Cotton. Pigs.

Much like gold, they went up in price a lot during the 1970s. In the 1980s and 1990s they went through a long period of low prices, but have gone up in price a lot this century. However, they're still volatile and subject to a lot of factors.

They had a big run up a few years ago, but crashed in 2008.

It's possible to trade contracts of these items on commodity exchanges. I feel about this pretty much as I do foreign exchange trading.

It's a great job if someone will pay you to trade with their money. If you have a run of good luck they'll love you and pay you a small fortune.

You can send your money into a commodities fund run by a Commodities Trading Adviser (CTA). I feel about this much as I do about hedge funds. They're a great way to make a small fortune - if you start with a large fortune.

If you have enough money, be my guest. You might get lucky.

The rest of us should stick with commodity Exchange Traded Funds.

And because pigs and bushels of wheat don't write checks, these ETFs don't pay dividends. So, again, you're going after capital gains.

Commodity prices will zoom up in the case of hyperinflation, yet drop down in the case of a deflationary depression.

For this list, I screened out non-U.S. ETFs. I screened out the ETFs going short. And I left out the ones using leverage.

Commodity ETFs

PowerShares DB Commodity Index Tracking Fund (DBC)

Dow Jones-AIG Commodity Index Total Return ETN (DJP)

E-TRACS Constant Maturity Commodity Index ETN (UCI)

E-TRACS DJ-UBS Commodity Index Total Return ETF (DJCI)

ELEMENTS Rogers International Commodity Index ETN (RJI)

ELEMENTS S&P Commodity Trends Indicator ETN (LSC)

Goldman Sachs Commodity Index (GSCI) Total Return Index ETN (GSP)

GreenHaven Continuous Commodity Index Fund (GCC)

GS Connect S&P GSCI Enhanced Commodity Total Return Strategy ETN (GSC)

iShares GSCI Commodity-Indexed Trust Fund (GSG)

PowerShares DB Commodity Long ETN (DPU)

PowerShares DB Agriculture Fund (DBA)

Dow Jones-AIG Agriculture Total Return ETN (JJA)

Dow Jones-AIG Copper Total Return ETN (JJC)

Dow Jones-AIG Energy Total Return ETN (JJE)

Dow Jones-AIG Grains Total Return ETN (JJG)

Dow Jones-AIG Industrial Metals Total Return ETN (JJM)

Dow Jones-AIG Livestock Total Return ETN (COW)

Dow Jones-AIG Nickel Total Return ETN (JJN)

E-TRACS CMCI Agriculture ETN (UAG)

E-TRACS CMCI Food ETN (FUD)

E-TRACS CMCI Industrial Metals ETN (UBM)

E-TRACS CMCI Livestock ETN (UBC)

E-TRACS CMCI Long Platinum ETN (PTM)

ELEMENTS MLCX Grains Index ETN (GRU)

ELEMENTS Rogers International Commodity - Agriculture Index ETN (RJA)

ELEMENTS Rogers International Commodity - Metals Index ETN (RJZ)

ETFS Physical Palladium Shares ETF (PALL)

ETFS Physical Platinum Shares ETF (PPLT)

iPath Dow Jones-AIG Aluminum Total Return Sub-Index ETN (JJU)

iPath Dow Jones-AIG Cocoa Total Return Sub-Index ETN (NIB)

iPath Dow Jones-AIG Coffee Total Return Sub-Index ETN (JO)

iPath Dow Jones-AIG Cotton Total Return Sub-Index ETN (BAL)

iPath Dow Jones-AIG Lead Total Return Sub-Index ETN (LD)

iPath Dow Jones-AIG Platinum Total Return Sub-Index ETN (PGM)

iPath Dow Jones-AIG Softs Total Return Sub-Index ETN (JJS)

iPath Dow Jones-AIG Sugar Total Return Sub-Index ETN (SGG)

iPath Dow Jones-AIG Tin Total Return Sub-Index ETN (JJT)

PowerShares DB Agriculture Long ETN (AGF)

PowerShares DB Base Metals Fund (DBB)

PowerShares DB Base Metals Long ETN (BDG)

Commodity Mutual Funds

Oppenheimer Real Asset Fund (QRACX)

PIMCO Commodity Real Return Strategy (PCRAX)

Which ones should you invest in?

My first recommendation is to say, none — because they don't pay dividends. You're better off letting a consumer product company buy the commodity and then transform it into a more profitable item.

Don't buy wheat and livestock, buy McDonald's.

Don't buy industrial metals, buy Gillette.

Don't buy sugar, buy Hershey.

However, commodities are closely linked to inflation, and I'm the only investment author who admits they're not a bonafide fortune teller. If you insist, buy these kinds of ETFs — but no more than 5% of your portfolio.

Chapter 11

Black Gold and the Latest Energy Crisis

If anything signifies the decline in the US dollar's purchasing power even more than gold, it's the price of oil.

Oil and energy of all kinds exploded in price during the 1970s, then drifted down again until they were low through the 1990s.

We know we're teetering on the brink of another oil crisis similar to 1973. If you're much younger than me, you probably don't know how we used to wait in line half an hour or longer to buy extremely expensive gasoline. In some areas the supply was controlled in ways similar to rationing.

Every president from Nixon to Obama has pledged to decrease our dependency on foreign oil, and every single one of them has broken that pledge. We're more dependent on foreign oil than we were in 1973. And it's obvious that's not about to change.

What's scary about oil is we could suffer a deflationary depression and could still — under the right conditions — see a huge rise in the price of oil.

Economic slowdowns generally lower the price of oil, but we also know it's hostage to events in the Mideast that could easily double or triple the price of a barrel of oil despite low demand.

Radical jihadists overthrowing the kingdom of Saudi Arabia.

A nuclear explosion anywhere in the Gulf Region.

Iran blocking the Gulf of Oman by using a missile to destroy an oil tanker in the Strait of Hormuz. (They recently ran a military exercise to practice doing that.)

The possibilities are many, but all of the good ones (peace between Israel and the Palestinians; a return to secular rule in Iran; the widespread MidEastern rejection of terrorists) seem improbable or far in the future.

Many experts claim the world is running out of oil. Other experts point out we keep discovering more. The problem is, the new oil is more difficult to reach and therefore more expensive.

So it does appear likely the price of energy is going up whether the United States government runs a budget deficit or surplus or whether or not we as a country keep our balance of trade balanced or whether or not we go back on the gold standard or whether or not other major world powers do any of those things.

To me, hedging your US dollar spending power with energy investments makes more sense than using gold.

We know energy is useful. Our entire civilization depends on it.

Oil is only good to be burned. No country keeps barrels of oil under lock and key in a Fort Knox. Nobody stores oil in their home safe. No ETF buys a bunch of oil and keeps it in storage.

No, we reserve such irrational behavior for gold. Gold is bright, shiny and beautiful. Oil is black, ugly and sticky. If we didn't need it we'd be glad to do without it.

Therefore, including some form of energy-related investments in your portfolio does seem to me prudent.

Chapter 11-A

Energy ETFs and Mutual Funds

For this list I screened out non-U.S. ETFs. I screened out the ETFs going short. And I left out the ones using leverage. I also screened out Exchange Traded Notes and limited partnerships. Those masquerade as ETFs, but they're not. They're effectively bonds with the risk the issuing company will fail.

PowerShares DB Energy Fund (NYSE Arca: DBE). Expenses 0.80%. No dividends. Tracks the Deutsche Bank Liquid Commodity Index - Optimum Yield Energy Excess Return™ ("DB Energy Index").

PowerShares DB Oil Fund (DBO). Expenses 0.75%. No dividends. Tracks the Deutsche Bank Liquid Commodity Index - Optimum Yield Oil Excess Return™ (the "DB Crude Oil Index").

SPDR S&P Oil & Gas Equipment & Services (NYSEArca: XES). Expenses 0.35%. Dividend: 3 cents per quarter. Tracks the S&P Oil & Gas Equipment & Services Select Industry® Index.

SPDR S&P Oil & Gas Exploration & Production (NYSEArca: XOP). Expenses 0.35%. Dividends: 1 cent per quarter. Tracks the S&P Oil & Gas Exploration & Production Select Industry® Index.

iShares Dow Jones U.S. Oil and Gas Exploration (NYSEArca: IEO). Expenses 0.47%. Dividends: 6.5 cents. Tracks the Dow Jones U.S. Select Oil Exploration & Production Index.

Claymore Natural Gas Commodity ETF (GAS-TSX). Expenses 0.80%. No dividends. Tracks the NGX Canadian Natural Gas Index

Claymore Oil Sands Sector ETF (CLO-TSX). Expenses: 0.60%. Dividends: 32 cents. Sustainable Oil Sands Sector Index™.

First Trust ISE-Revere Natural Gas Index Fund (FCG). Expenses: 0.60%. No dividends. Tracks the ISE-Revere Natural Gas IndexTM.

If you wish to feel good about investing in alternative energy, try this ETF on wind power:

Global Wind Energy Portfolio ETF (PWND). Expenses 0.75%. No dividends. Tracks the NASDAQ OMX Clean Edge® Global Wind Energy Index.

Some of these hold stocks in energy companies. Some of them use futures contracts to replicate the market performance.

To me the clear winner is XES, for three reasons.

1. It has low expenses.

2. It pays a dividend.

3. It invests in companies supplying energy infrastructure so it's not dependent on the market price of energy.

The exploration ETFs are risky. The companies they hold may not find much oil even though the price is $1,000 per barrel.

I personally prefer for the underlying companies to prove themselves to be long-term dividend payers. Then they will make the Mergent Dividend Achievers indexes. Then I'll own them through that ETF.

If you wish a straight energy play to hedge the price of gasoline at the pump or your home heating bill, buying DBE is the most direct way to do that.

Energy Mutual Funds

Vanguard Energy (VGENX). Expenses 0.38%. No loads. Annual dividends $0.9190.

Guinness Atkinson Global Energy Fund (GAGEX). Expenses 1.31%. No dividends.

BlackRock Energy & Resources(SSGRX). Expenses 1.31%. No dividends.

Waddell & Reed Energy(WEGAX). Expenses 1.83%. No

dividends.

Franklin Natural Resources(FRNRX). Expenses 1.09%. Annual dividends $0.4289.

I'm sure there are others.

My rule of thumb regarding mutual funds and ETFs is if Vanguard has what I'm looking for, that's the one I buy. Vanguard Energy has the clear advantage of low expenses and paying dividends. Unfortunately, it also requires a minimum of $25,000 to open an account. So I included some alternatives.

New Alternatives Fund (NALFX) invests in socially responsible alternative energy, including natural gas. Therefore it's not a short-term hedge against rising oil prices, but in twenty or thirty years it may help save the world.

There are three other ways to invest in energy, both of which, as an income investor, I heartily approve of:

Canadian income former trusts now corporations

Master Limited Partnerships

Utilities

Chapter 11-B

Canadian Energy Companies

In Canada The Income Tax Act of 1985 created a new form of business structure, the publicly traded business trust.

These were managed by a trustee, but owned by unit holders who could buy and sell their units on the secondary market just as though they were shares of stock.

If the trust paid out at least 90% of net profits to the unit holders, it owed no income taxes.

The main intent of this law was to encourage development of the country's natural resources. Therefore, although some Canadian business trusts were in other areas (for example: Canada's Yellow Pages and Canada's A&W Root Beer), most such trusts operated in natural resources. Some of them in mining, many in oil and natural gas exploration and drilling.

Unfortunately, the Canadian government has rescinded the tax-favored status of these trusts. Effective 2011, they must pay taxes as corporations. This will reduce some of their benefit for us income investors. Most have converted back to corporation status.

The good news is many still pay high dividends.

They are still developing Canada's badly needed energy resources. If they're well-run and own valuable properties, they should continue to make a lot of profit, especially if the price of energy and other commodities keeps going up.

From a foreign exchange viewpoint, owning them is an indirect way of profiting from the rise of the Canadian dollar against the US dollar.

You can profit from owning them even if their price — in Canadian dollars — doesn't change.

Guggenheim Canadian Energy Income ETF (NYSE Arca: ENY). Expenses 0.65%. Dividends: $0.105. Tracks the Sustainable Canadian Energy Income Index. This includes Canadian oil and gas producers.

Top Ten Holdings

Cenovus Energy Inc
Suncor Energy Inc
Imperial Oil Ltd
Canadian Natural Resource
Meg Energy Corporation
Canadian Oil Sands Ltd
Baytex Energy Corp
Southern Pacific Resource Co
Blackpearl Resources Inc
Athabasca Oil Sands Corporation

We want Canadian energy (in whatever business structure) and a hedge against the Canadian dollar, and ENY delivers them both. With low expenses and a dividend to boot.

Chapter 11-C

Master Limited Partnerships

Master Limited Partnerships, I believe, are one of the best income investments available today and one of the best ways to take advantage of our civilization's dependence on energy.

I believe in them so strongly I wrote an entire book — Master Limited Partnerships — about them. If you want more information, I suggest you check it out.

Master Limited Partnerships are not a direct hedge on rising energy prices. In a way, they're better. The type of MLPs I recommend ("midstream") make money from energy use, not from its market price.

Therefore, well-run MLPs are profitable whether oil is $10 a barrel or $1,000 a barrel. However, I must admit although society is always going to need to use a minimum level of income, actual use can fluctuate.

Many MLPs lost business during the 2008-2009 economic crisis. Almost all of them remained profitable, but it's possible if we're hit with an extreme energy crisis and we can't even afford to drive our cars, MLP distributions could go down.

"Midstream" means the part of the petroleum process we usually don't think about.

We focus on the beginning — oil wells — and the end — what we pay for a gallon of gasoline — and take for granted the infrastructure that connects them.

MLPs are a Great "Tollbooth" Business

Midstreams MLPs own the pipes, storage facilities, terminals and refineries which connect newly pumped oil and gas to the end users (utility companies and us).

They get paid an amount set by the government to transport oil and natural gas. The government's regulatory agency increases the price they can charge every July by the Producer Price Index (PPI) — the business equivalent of the Consumer Price Index to measure inflation — plus 1.3%.

Therefore, MLP income goes up by more than inflation.

So long as MLPs pay out at least 90% of their cash to their limited partners (you and I), they don't have to pay federal taxes. So their quarterly distributions historically yield around 7%.

Even better, because much of that cash flow represents "return of capital" for equipment depreciation, an average of 80% or more of that cash is tax-deferred until you sell your trust units.

Which, therefore, I advise you to never do.

On average, their quarterly distributions go up around 9% per year. This average went down in 2009 because of the recession, but MLPs suffered a lot less than other financial securities.

MLPs are Almost But Not Quite Perfect

MLPs have three major drawbacks.

One is, because you're a limited partner and not a corporate shareholder, at the end of the year you receive K-1 partnership reporting forms instead of W-2 forms.

They are more complicated, but almost all MLPs allow you to download the information through Turbo Tax, and good tax preparers should be able to handle it for you.

Plus, though I'm reluctant to recommend them because they use leverage, you can buy MLPs through closed-end funds.

Number two is, because of their structure, they should not be held directly in tax-deferred retirement accounts.

However, you can put the closed-end funds in your IRA. And two MLPs allow you to buy i-units, which issue distributions in the form of additional partnership units.

Number Three is, due again to their structure, you cannot buy any ETFs — my preferred form of financial security — holding MLPs. Mutual funds are allowed to own up to 25% of their assets as MLPs but, due to some technical practical issues, they don't.

Therefore, you must hold the partnership units directly. Or buy leveraged closed-end funds. Or buy i-units.

MLP I-Units

Kinder Morgan Management, LLC (NYSE: KMR)

Enbridge Energy Management, L.L.C. (NYSE: EEQ)

You'll notice these are limited liability companies (LLCs) not limited partnerships. You're buying units of memberships in them. That's the point. They hold limited partnership units in Kinder Morgan Energy Partners, L.P. (NYSE: KMP) and Enbridge Energy Partners, L.P. (NYSE: EEP) respectively.

Every quarter, they then issue additional membership shares to you based on the quarterly distributions of the MLPs.

It's in effect a form of Dividend Re-Investment Program (DRIP).

Yes, it's convoluted accounting, and it's available only for those two companies, but it allows you to profit from them in a tax-deferred account or without having to deal with a K-1 form at tax time.

MLP Closed-End Funds

Cushing MLP Total Return Fund (NYSE:SRV)

Energy Income & Growth (FEN)

Fiduciary/Claymore MLP (FMO)

Kayne Anderson Energy Development Company (KED)

Kayne Anderson MLP (KYN)

MLP & Strategic Equity Fund Inc (MTP)

Tortoise Capital Resources (TTO)

Tortoise Energy (TYY)

Tortoise Energy Infrastructure (TYG)

Tortoise North American Energy Corp. (NYSE: TYN)

Kayne Anderson Energy Total (KYE)

I'm leery of these because they do use leverage or other derivatives to enhance returns, but you can buy them for a tax-deferred account or just to simplify your taxes.

Individual Midstream MLPs

Atlas Pipeline Partners, L.P. (AMEX: APL)

Atlas Pipeline Holdings, L.P. (AMEX: AHD)

Boardwalk Pipeline Partners, L.P. (NYSE: BWP)

Buckeye Partners, L.P. (NYSE: BPL)

Buckeye GP Holdings, L.P. (NYSE: BGH)

Calumet Specialty Products Partners, L.P. (NASDAQ: CLMT)

Cheniere Energy Partners, L.P. (AMEX: CQP)

Crosstex Energy, L.P. (NASDAQ: XTEX)

DCP Midstream Partners, L.P (NYSE: DPM)

Duncan Energy Partners, L.P. (NYSE: DEP)

Eagle Rock Energy Partners, L.P. (NASDAQ: EROC)

El Paso Pipeline Partners, L.P. (NYSE: EPB)

Enbridge Energy Partners, L.P. (NYSE: EEP)

Energy Transfer Partners, L.P. (NYSE: ETP)

Energy Transfer Equity, L.P. (NYSE: ETE)

Enterprise Products Partners, L.P. (NYSE: EPD)

Enterprise GP Holdings, L.P. (NYSE: EPE)

Exterran Partners, L.P. (NASDAQ: EXLP)

Genesis Energy, L.P. (AMEX: GEL)

Holly Energy Partners, L.P. (NYSE: HEP)

Kinder Morgan Energy Partners, L.P. (NYSE: KMP)

Magellan Midstream Partners, L.P. (NYSE: MMP)

MarkWest Energy Partners, L.P. (AMEX: MWE)

Nustar Energy, L.P. (NYSE: NS)

NuStar GP Holdings, L.P. (NYSE: NSH)

ONEOK Partners, L.P. (NYSE: OKS)

Plains All American Pipeline, L.P. (NYSE: PAA)

Quicksilver Gas Services, L.P. (NYSE: KGS)

Regency Energy Partners LP (NASDAQ: RGNC)

Spectra Energy Partners, L.P. (NYSE: SEP)

Sunoco Logistics Partners, L.P. (NYSE: SXL)

Targa Resources Partners, L.P. (NASDAQ: NGLS)

TC Pipelines, L.P. (NASDAQ: TCLP)

TransMontaigne Partners, L.P. (NYSE: TLP)

Western Gas Partners, L.P. (NYSE: WES)

Williams Partners, L.P. (NYSE: WPZ)

Williams Pipeline Partners, L.P. (NYSE: WMZ)

If you're buying for a taxable account, I suggest you buy a broad range of these and use some of your extra quarterly income to pay an accountant to do your taxes.

Remember, MLPs make money so long as somebody is buying

oil and natural gas.

Many of those customers are utility companies.

Chapter 11-D

Utilities

Utility companies supply basic needs to household and businesses — water, electricity, communications and natural gas.

It's estimated in the future electricity will be a scarcer resource than oil. Building electric power plants of all types is a major priority for China.

Still Good for Widows and Orphans — and the Rest of Us Too

So my conclusion is — utility companies are businesses that are not going away because they supply basic human needs. Here in the U.S. and in other countries as well.

Utility companies have traditionally paid good dividends — they're the archetypal "widows and orphans" stock because they're considered so safe.

This would not be possible if utility companies had to compete as most other companies do. Because they are dependent on spending large amount of money for power plants, wiring and so on, most of their earnings would normally be reinvested in maintaining and expanding their capital equipment.

However, utility companies are regulated monopolies. This means they are assured of a customer base, which must buy from them. The government agencies that regulate them are supposed to allow them to charge those customers for all their legitimate expenses, plus make a reasonable profit.

Therefore, well-run and well-regulated utilities make enough money to finance their ongoing need for capital to build new power plants and whatever else they need, and also pay a generous dividend to their shareholders.

Unless We Return to a Pre-Industrial Agriculture Society, We'll Need Utility Companies

Despite all economic problems, demand for electricity and natural gas will continue to increase. People will continue to pay their utility bills. And so utilities will continue to reward investors with ongoing income.

However, if we reach a crisis and energy becomes extremely expensive, the agencies that regulate utilities will come under intense political pressure not to allow them the rate hikes they'll seek.

Therefore, utilities are not a complete hedge against an energy crisis.

However, they are powerful, so foreign utility company stocks are one way to protect yourself against a weak US dollar. They'll continue to send you dividend checks from all major world currencies.

Utility Companies Outside the U.S. ETFs

1. SPDR S&P International Utilities Sector ETF (IPU)

Tracks the S&P Developed Ex-U.S. BMI Utilities Sector Index, an index that tracks the utilities sector of developed global markets outside the United States. Expense ratio is 0.5%. Dividends: $0.019240.

2. WisdomTree International Utilities Sector Fund (DBU)

Expenses 0.58%. It concentrates on Europe, but includes Japan, Hong Kong and China. It does include the United States, but only 0.14%. That's small enough to be insignificant.

(Besides, owning US utilities is good. It's just here we're trying to hedge against the US dollar so we want dividends denominated in other currencies.)

Dividends: $0.02467.

3. S&P Global Utilities Sector Index Fund (JXI)

Tracks the S&P Global Utilities Index. Expense ratio is 0.48% and it holds 76 companies in the developed world, with about 1/3 U.S. companies.

We can ignore JXI because it's one-third U.S. utility companies.

It's a close call between IPU and DBU. Both include high quality utilities around the world. DBU's expense ratio is slightly higher.

Both pay dividends, so I'd have to say to go with the one with the higher yield. That will vary every day with their market prices so you'll just have to compare them.

Next: protecting our purchasing power the direct way — owning other currencies.

Chapter 12

Owning Other Currencies

The most direct way of protecting our purchasing power against the decline of the US dollar relative to other currencies is simply to own money denominated in the other currencies.

That's obvious, yet not so easy.

You could fly to other countries (drive to Canada), exchange your US dollars for their money, then bring the cash back with you.

They may frown on you doing that in large quantities. When I was leaving India, I upset a government official by keeping about five dollars' worth of rupees in my wallet.

However, you can't spend it in businesses in America (with the exception of stores close to the northern border that accept Canadian money). You can take it to a bank, but most American banks charge outrageous fees to convert foreign currency and use rip-off exchange rates.

When I first went to Thailand twenty years ago, currency exchange was fast, professional and carried out at close to wholesale banking rates. In Manila money changing is still a mom and pop operation, but it's highly competitive so rates are high as they can be, and they don't charge extra fees. I wish banks in the United States could be half so advanced.

But they're not, so I can't advise you to hold foreign currency in the form of cash.

You could fly to other countries, exchange your dollars for their currency and then open a bank account in that country to keep the money in.

If you want to take more than $10,000 out of the U.S. you must declare it, or our government will assume you're a drug dealer and confiscate the money.

Also, the other country may have laws, restrictions and requirements about who they allow to open bank accounts in their country.

And you have to declare foreign bank accounts to the IRS or they'll assume you're trying to evade paying taxes.

And how will it be to get money wired from your Parisian or London or Tokyo bank account if you're back home in Wisconsin when the US dollar hits the fan?

You can own foreign currency ETFs or certificates of deposit denominated in foreign currencies.

Chapter 12-A

Foreign Currency ETFs

Again, I screened out non-U.S. based ETFs, ETNs, ETFs using leverage, one fund long the US dollar (that's for foreigners who need to hedge their own currency, not for us Americans who are already long the dollar through our jobs and incomes), and one fund arbitraging interest rates.

Major Currency ETFs

CurrencyShares Australian Dollar Trust ETF (FXA)

CurrencyShares British Pound Sterling Trust ETF (FXB)

CurrencyShares Canadian Dollar Trust ETF (FXC)

CurrencyShares Euro Trust ETF (FXE)

CurrencyShares Japanese Yen Trust ETF (FXY)

CurrencyShares Swedish Krona Trust ETF (FXS)

CurrencyShares Swiss Franc Trust ETF (FXF)

WisdomTree Dreyfus Euro Fund (EU)

WisdomTree Dreyfus Japanese Yen Fund (JYF)

WisdomTree Dreyfus New Zealand Dollar Fund (BNZ)

Barclays Asian and Gulf Currency Revaluation ETN (PGD)

There are ETFs tracking the performance of emerging currencies, but that's a form of gambling, not a way to hedge your US dollar risk.

It'd be nice if an ETF company would put together one ETF that tracks all major currencies except the US dollar. So that, by buying one ETF, you could obtain the benefit of owning Australian dollars, British pounds, euros, Japanese yen, Swiss francs, Singapore dollars, Hong Kong dollars, Canadian dollars and New Zealand dollars.

Unfortunately, to obtain that across-the-board protection you must now buy some of each of the above ETFs.

Wouldn't it be easier just to own certificates of deposit on foreign currencies, so we'd receive interest income and have them conveniently close by?

Chapter 12-B

Foreign Currency Certificates of Deposit

Check out Everbank at

http://www.everbank.com/001Currency.aspx

Although located in the United States and accessible online, Everbank offers you the opportunity to own certificates of deposits in seventeen different foreign currencies. Many of the CDs are a combination of currencies.

You can open a CD in these single currencies:

Australian dollars
Brazilian reals
British pounds
Canadian dollars
Czech koruna
Danish krone
Euros
Hong Kong dollars
Indian rupees

Japanese yen
Mexican pesos
New Zealand dollars
Norwegian krone
Singapore dollars
South African rand
Swedish kronas
Swiss francs

I'm listing what's available, not necessarily what's advisable. I'd stick with the Australian dollar, British pound, Canadian dollar, Danish krone, euro, Japanese yen, Hong Kong dollars, Singapore dollars, New Zealand dollar, Swedish krona and Swiss franc.

However, the interest rate you'll earn depends on what's available in their countries. Therefore, they're mostly low. And the Swiss franc, Japanese yen and Swedish krona CDs pay no interest. Until market interest rates in those countries go up, you're depending for a return on their value to go up against the US dollar.

They each have a $10,000 minimum.

CD Baskets

They each have a $20,000 minimum.

Commodity Basket CD

Australian dollar
Canadian dollar
New Zealand dollar

South African rand

Debt-Free Basket CD

Australian dollar
Brazilian real
Japanese yen
Singapore dollar
Swiss franc

Euro Trax® Basket CD

Euro
Norwegian krone
Swedish krona
Swiss franc

European Opportunity Basket CD

Hungarian forint
Polish zloty
Czech koruna

Geographic Basket CD

Australian dollar
Euro
Hong Kong dollar
Mexican peso

Global Power ShiftSM Basket CD

Australian dollar
Brazilian real
Canadian dollar
Norwegian krone

Investor's Opportunity Basket CD

Mexican peso
Australian dollar
Euro
New Zealand dollar

New World EnergySM Basket CD

Australian dollar
Canadian dollar
Norwegian krone

Pacific Advantage® Basket CD

New Zealand dollar
Hong Kong dollar
Japanese yen
Singapore dollar

Pan-AsianSM Basket CD

Australian dollar
Hong Kong dollar
Japanese yen
Singapore dollar

Petrol Basket CD

British pound
Mexican peso
Norwegian krone

Prudent Central Bank Basket CD

Australian dollar
British pound
Euro
New Zealand dollar

Ultra Resource Basket CD

Australian dollar
Hong Kong dollar
Canadian dollar
New Zealand dollar
Norwegian krone
Singapore dollar

Viking Basket CD

Norwegian krone
Danish krone
Swedish krona

World Energy Basket CD

Australian dollar
British pound
Canadian dollar
Norwegian krone

Unfortunately, Everbank doesn't offer a single "all major foreign currencies and only major foreign currencies" basket. It mingles developed currencies with developing currencies.

Therefore, I suggest the EuroTrax, Pan-Asian or Pacific Advantage and World Energy baskets CDs.

You can also open a money market account at Everbank and hold it in the form of a foreign currency. The minimum deposit is $2,500, but if you deposit at least $10,000 you earn interest on the foreign currency.

Certificates of deposit hold short-term notes and commercial paper. This makes them safe but, remember, in a deflationary depression some debtors — including previously creditworthy individuals and businesses — will be unable to pay their debts.

Therefore, these CDs are not as safe as cash. But they're better than you flying to all those countries to open up savings accounts.

Just remember if the sky seems to be falling across the entire world, rather than just in the United States, to convert these accounts to cash in US dollars. If another currency seems stronger than the US dollar, convert your money into a certificate of that particular currency.

Chapter 13

Foreign Bonds

Another way to own foreign currencies is in the form of bonds. The market value of the bonds will go up if the US dollar goes down, and we receive interest income denominated in a foreign currency.

Until recently, government (or sovereign) bonds from most developed countries were considered as safe as US Treasuries. Now, according to Standard & Poor's, the US government has a credit rating of only AA, down from AAA. Many other countries, especially in Europe, are also getting downgraded. Greece, Italy, Spain, Portugal and Ireland are widely considered at great risk of defaulting.

And that should be a warning. Bonds are often recommended as a hedge against deflation because they go up in value when interest rates fall.

That's true if we have just a small amount of deflation. And these investments will protect your purchasing power from a decline in the US dollar so long as the rest of the world's economies remain strong.

Remember, however, bonds are a form of I.O.U. And the whole purpose of deflationary depressions is to squeeze debt out of the economy.

If there's a general crash, therefore, many debtors will not repay their debts. It now appears that will include some foreign corporations and governments.

That's why I recommend Exchange Traded Funds, so you get a broad diversification.

The situation with Greece shows, whatever we think about current levels of US government spending, other countries also have major problems.

Sovereign Bond ETFs

SPDR Capital International Treasury Bond ETF (BWX)

This ETF tracks the Barclays Capital Global Treasury ex-US Capped Index. It covers fixed-rate local currency sovereign debt of investment grade countries outside of the US, in local currencies, with a remaining period of one year or more.

SPDR Barclays Capital Short-Term International Treasury Bond ETF (BWZ)

Tracks the Barclays Capital 1-3 Year Global Treasury ex-US Capped Index. This ETF is much like BWX, though limited to bonds with 1-3 years remaining until maturity.

iShares S&P / Citi International Treasury Bond ETF (IGOV)

This tracks the S&P/Citigroup International Treasury Bond Index Ex-US index.

iShares S&P / Citi 1-3 Year International Treasury Bond ETF (ISHG)

Tracks the S&P/Citigroup International Treasury Bond Index Ex-US 1-3 Year index. Again, much like IGOV, but with holdings of shorter duration and therefore less risky.

My suggestion is to stick to the shorter term ETFs — BWX and ISHG. They'll be less risky in the event of deflation. You'll sacrifice a little bit of yield, because longer term bonds pay a higher rate of interest, but the extra risk isn't worth it. And you'll still have income-producing assets denominated outside the US dollar.

Foreign Corporate Bonds ETFs

Barclays Capital International Corporate Bond ETF (IBND)

This ETF is brand new. It tracks the Barclays Capital Global Aggregate ex-USD >$1B: Corporate Bond Index. Securities must be investment grade according to at least two ratings agencies, have a minimum $1 billion market capitalization and have at least one year remaining until maturity.

This will have a higher yield than the sovereign bond ETFs, but are riskier, so load up on BWX and ISHG first.

Chapter 14

Foreign Stocks

To my mind, foreign stocks that pay dividends are the number one way of protecting your purchasing power unless there's an absolute worldwide across-the-board catastrophe.

Their market price will fluctuate in the local currency, but will effectively go up if the US dollar declines.

However, their market price could go down farther than the dollar, in which case you've lost money.

But at least you receive income denominated in that currency through the company's business activity.

However, you must remember buying stocks is profitable only in the long run.

The basic types of stocks to buy are:

1. Ordinary consumer brand stocks that pay dividends.

2. Real Estate Investment Trusts

3. Utilities

We've covered #3 in an earlier chapter.

Also, to protect yourself with diversification, buy only Exchange Traded Funds. Don't try to buy individual foreign stocks whether you use a local brokerage, American Deposit Receipts (ADRs) or pink sheets.

Foreign Companies that Pay Dividends ETFs

1. PowerShares International Dividend Achievers Portfolio: PID

This tracks the Mergent International Dividend Achievers Index. That is, these are the stocks of companies outside the U.S. with a history of raising their dividends every year for at least five years.

2. WisdomTree DEFA Fund: DWM

This tracks the WisdomTree Dividend Index of Europe, Far East Asia and Australasia (DEFA).

3. WisdomTree DEFA Equity Income Fund: DTH

The WisdomTree DEFA Equity Index consists of the companies in the WisdomTree DEFA Index with the highest dividend yields.

Here, my vote is for PID, since it takes any company outside the U.S. so long as it's raised its dividends every year for at least 5 years. DTH is a close second since it tracks the companies currently paying the highest dividends.

Foreign REIT ETFs

1. SPDR DJ Wilshire International Real Estate ETF (RWX)

Tracks the Dow Jones Global ex-U.S. Select Real Estate Securities Index. Expenses 0.59%. Dividends $0.157176.

2. S&P Developed ex-U.S. Property Index Fund (WPS)

Tracks the S&P/ Developed ex-U.S Property Index. Expenses 0.48%. Dividends $0.20668.

3. WisdomTree International Real Estate Fund (DRW)

Tracks the WisdomTree International Real Estate Index. Expenses 0.58%. Dividends $0.1635.

At last count, nearly 40 countries in the world besides the US have REITs or REIT-like laws. That means these ETFs probably overlap quite a bit, so buy just one.

WPS has the lowest expense ratio.

When you're ready to buy, figure out which has the highest yield and go with that.

Chapter 15

Treasury Inflation Protected Securities — Foreign and Domestic

These are government-issued bonds deliberately designed to help protect you from inflation.

Of course, that means they're complicated and come with a catch.

When they're issued they have a normal par value of $1,000, with a lower than market rate of interest.

Every year until maturity, the principal of the bond is increased by the amount of annual inflation as defined by the government's Consumer Price Index for Urban Workers (CPI-U).

The coupon interest rate remains constant.

Thus, if inflation is 3.5% in its first year, after that year the principal amount of a $1,000 face value TIP bond becomes $1,035, and your interest payment is the rate times $1,035 instead of $1,000.

The interest payments are made every six months.

You Do Pay for This Inflation-Fighting Guarantee With a Small Yield

One disadvantage to these bonds is their interest rate is fairly low, to pay for this inflation protection. Thus, if inflation remains low during the lifetime of the bond, you'd have done better to buy another type of bond.

An ever bigger disadvantage is you must pay federal income taxes on the interest and the inflation adjusted amount - even though you don't actually receive the cash for them until the bond matures, which could be 20 years from now.

Therefore, in the example above, you would have to report that $35 increase in your bond's face value on your tax return, and pay taxes on it as well as on the interest you received.

But notice that $35 is not in your pocket - you won't actually receive it for another 19 years.

It may seem unfair to pay taxes on money you won't receive for up to 19 years, but that one of the prices you pay for inflation protection.

However, the interest from TIPS is excluded from local and state taxes.

If deflation occurs, the TIPS bond principal goes down. At the end of twenty years, you receive the adjusted or original principal, whichever is higher.

Investors Not Yet Retired Should Hold TIPS Only in Tax-Deferred Retirement Accounts

If you are still saving for retirement, you should hold TIPS only in tax-deferred accounts such as IRAs. That way you don't have to pay any taxes on the phantom income.

If you're already retired, there is a way to own TIPS outside a tax-deferred account without paying taxes on the phantom income.

That's to buy shares of the **iShares Barclays Treasury Inflation Protected Securities Bond Fund (TIP).** This fund buys up issues of TIPS bonds to track the Barclays Capital U.S. Treasury Inflation Protected Securities (TIPS) Index (Series-L).

Their expense ratio is only 0.20%. Their dividends are quite irregular, however, and sometimes aren't paid for months.

Other countries have also come up with bonds to protect against inflation.

The United Kingdom began issuing "Inflation-linked Gilts" (ILGs) in 1981. In 1991 Canada issued "Real Return Bond" (RRBs). Sweden, France, Japan, Mexico, Turkey, Germany, Australia, New Zealand and many other governments also issue inflation-linked bonds.

You can profit from them by buying shares of:

SPDR DB International Government Inflation Protected Bond ETF (WIP)

Tracks the DB Global Government ex-US Inflation-Linked Bond Capped Index, which includes the TIPS-equivalents of eighteen other countries.

However, dividend payments from this fund are irregular.

This fund protects your purchasing power by firing from both barrels:

1. You own income-producing assets denominated in foreign currencies.

2. These assets are designed to go up in value to the extent the issuing country's economy suffers from inflation.

When I examined all the other major world currencies and their prospects, I came to the conclusion the one most likely to prosper in the future no matter what happens to the world's economy was the Swiss franc.

Is there some high quality investment denominated in the Swiss franc?

Chapter 16

Swiss Annuities

Get Your Variable Annuities From the World's Safest Life Insurance Companies, and Put Them in What May Be the World's Safest Form of Money

(NOTE: in my book Income Investing Secrets I have a VERY long chapter on fixed and variable annuities. I'm not repeating those technicalities here. Let me just say variable annuities are a way of investing through insurance companies. They may be appropriate for you if you've maxed out your tax-deferred accounts, want to shelter additional investment earnings from taxes and have a long time-line. With Swiss annuities you get the tax advantages of U.S. variables annuities and can put your money in high quality Swiss investments denominated in the Swiss franc.)

What if you could get all the benefits of fixed and variable annuities AND —

1. You could choose from among the life insurance companies with the highest credit ratings in the world? Since 1885, no

company in this group has ever failed. (Prominent American and British life insurance companies have gone out of business.)

2. You could elect to hold your investments in your choice of the euro, the British pound or the Swiss franc?

3. You would have almost ironclad protection against creditors and lawsuits?

4. It was up to you to notify the IRS and pay taxes on your taxable income proceeds (when you take them)?

All these benefits are available through investing in Swiss annuities.

No, not Swiss bank accounts.

Let's get THAT out of the way right up front. I'm NOT advising you to open up a Swiss bank account, certainly not one of the infamous "numbered" accounts so beloved of thriller novelists.

Swiss bank accounts have to be reported to the IRS on your annual 1040 or on Treasury form 90-22.1. Swiss annuities don't have to be declared. However, when you start to draw out earnings, they are taxable in the U.S. and should therefore go on your 1040. You are not required to report to the U.S. government the mere ownership of a foreign life insurance policy or annuity.

Plus, the Swiss government requires foreigners to pay an onerous 35% tax on bank account earnings. This is not true of Swiss annuities.

Switzerland Has Long Been Renowned for Quality and Safety

Switzerland has a long-standing reputation for quality and safety.

The Swiss traditionally value hard work for the creation of wealth, and privacy. They abhor welfare and debt — personal and governmental (a law was once proposed to give the government the authority to operate at a budget deficit — the law was voted down by the people). They believe in low taxes and a decentralized government.

The Swiss are the Traditional "Squares" You Want Guarding Your Money

They exemplify traditional, conservative, Republican virtues. That may personally appeal to you or horrify you. But whether you're a Republican, Democrat or Libertarian when it comes to American politics, you can take advantage of the Swiss system for your own financial benefit.

Swiss Life Insurance Companies Have the Best Track Record of Safety in the World

Through the Swiss Federal Office of Private Insurance (FOPI), the Swiss government has regulated Swiss life insurance companies since 1885, requiring the highest standards. Since the first Swiss life insurance company was founded in 1857, none have ever declared bankruptcy.

Swiss life insurance companies invest in blue chip bonds, preferred stocks, Swiss real estate and first mortgages.

In addition to the tax-deferral of the investment earnings on your contributions, Swiss annuities offer these advantages:

1. You can diversify into the Swiss franc, euro, and/or pounds sterling.

2. Asset protection and financial privacy

Swiss annuities taken out in Switzerland are governed by Swiss law. Swiss law places primary importance on people taking care of their families. Therefore, if the beneficiary of your annuity is a spouse or a descendant (child, grandchild and so on), creditors cannot touch it.

Also, creditors cannot touch your annuity if your beneficiary is someone else, but you've made an irrevocable election. That is, you've made a friend, cousin or anyone else your beneficiary, and that cannot be changed.

By the way, you must take out the Swiss annuity 1 year prior to any lawsuit or bankruptcy proceedings, and it must not have been done with the intent to defraud creditors. (The burden of proof is on your creditors to convince a Swiss court you did have intent to defraud them.)

Also, the contract or policy must be physically deposited in Switzerland.

Also, if you are declared bankrupt by a court, according to Swiss law, your annuity ownership transfers to the beneficiary — not to your creditors.

Swiss annuities protect your assets in other ways.

Your ownership of them is private. If you're in the accumulation stage, there's no American financial record of it. Even if you're drawing income, the only record of it is on your tax return, which the IRS is supposed to keep private. If you're sued, how is the lawyer opposing you going to even know you own one (assuming you keep your mouth shut)?

If the lawyer does learn you have a Swiss annuity, they're not likely to fly to Switzerland, hire a Swiss attorney and take your case to Swiss court — unless they think they can win an awful lot of money from you.

3. More lenient surrender policies than American variable annuity contracts

A Swiss annuity typically charges you a penalty for early withdrawal only in the first 1-3 years of the policy. Plus, they charge lower M & E fees than American annuity companies.

Also, you can borrow up to 90% of the value of your contract, so Swiss annuities are far more liquid than those offered by American life insurance companies.

4. No excise tax for Americans

Americans can take out annuities from other foreign life insurance companies, but then you must pay a 1% excise tax. Thanks to the 1998 U.S./Swiss Double Tax Treaty amendment, Americans don't have to pay that 1% excise tax on Swiss annuities.

5. Extreme financial security

Swiss life insurance companies are required to maintain a separate reserve account for every annuity. If they had to, they could meet all their financial responsibilities by issuing checks tomorrow.

Disadvantages

1. When you choose to receive immediate annuity payments, you can choose only annual, semiannual or quarterly payments. Monthly checks are reserved for Swiss residents.

2. The minimum amount you can start a Swiss annuity with is around $US 25,000 per currency selected. The minimum subsequent deposit allowed is usually around $US 10,000.

3. It's my understanding if you choose a Swiss fixed annuity, under U.S. law, you get no tax-deferral of the earnings on your investment, even if actual payment is deferred. That's because a foreign fixed annuity contract is considered an original issue discount debt instrument.

However, Swiss variable annuities still qualify for tax-deferral, because the life insurance aspect makes them not a debt instrument. Therefore, U.S. citizens and residents should consider accumulating assets only in Swiss variable annuities — not fixed annuities.

Swiss variable annuities qualify for U.S. tax deferral only if they're NOT "self-directed." If they are, there is no tax deferral. This is not a big deal, because NO American variable annuities are self-directed.

The U.S. government outlawed annuity contract owners investing in individual securities. So you must allow the Swiss company to control your investments, but you can still choose the subaccounts, so long as it's at least five, same as for American variable annuity contracts.

Check with your tax adviser for more details.

4. The additional costs of these investments may reduce their total returns, so you must weigh the advantages and disadvantages carefully.

Don't Be Fooled Into Thinking You Can Buy a Swiss Annuity in the U.S. or Canada — You Can't

Make sure your annuity is really a Swiss annuity — that is, governed by Swiss law.

There're Swiss life insurance companies operating inside the United States that will be glad to sell you annuities — but since they're operating within the U.S., they're governed by U.S. law.

You must take out the annuity directly from a Swiss life insurance company in Switzerland or Bermuda. You can do this by mail or by flying to one of these places if you choose. Make sure that the company signs the contract in Switzerland or Bermuda.

Variable annuities from any country are not for everybody.

But if variable annuities are a worthwhile investment for you, put at least 25% of your annuity money into Swiss annuities.

Section Three

Your Personal Finances

Chapter 17

Make an Investment Plan

I bet you didn't realize you could protect your US dollar purchasing power in so many ways, did you?

Now comes the hard part — making a coherent plan.

Now bear in mind I don't know anything about you or your finances. I don't know how old you are. I don't know your income. I don't know how much you have saved or what your current portfolio is. I don't know whether or not you're retired yet.

I'm not a certified financial adviser. What I write here are my generic opinions. I'm not qualified to give personal financial advice. And I'm not doing so.

You should run all this information by your professional financial adviser.

It's the responsibility of you and your financial adviser to adapt this information to your unique, particular individual or family situation.

You must also decide what your goals and time-line are.

Do you just want to add some inflation hedge to your current portfolio?

Are you scared but have little money to invest?

If the dollar shoots up in value next month are you going to want to undo everything and buy US stocks?

How much money do you have to invest?

Are you using an IRA or not? (Before you make any other kind of investments, you should max out all possible tax-deferred accounts.)

Personally, I follow the system I describe in Income Investing Secrets, which includes buying both U.S. and non-U.S. income investments. Thanks to the research I did for this book, as time goes by I'll be including some additional investments. But all of them will pay out some income.

However, maybe you're comfortable investing for market price appreciation, especially against the US dollar.

You must also think about whether you're scared of inflation, deflation or both.

As I've tried to make clear as I've gone along, some investments are good for protecting against inflation and some are good for protecting against deflation.

And neither you nor I nor anybody else in the world know which one will be the big problem.

Therefore, I'm recommending a broad range of both types.

When you don't know the future (which we never do), protect yourself through diversification.

Here — in no particular order — are what I'd say are the most important ways to protect your purchasing power:

1. Master Limited Partnerships

2. Foreign stocks ETFs (including foreign REIT ETFs)

3. TIPS (including the foreign TIPS ETF)

4. Foreign bonds

5. Energy ETFs (including ETFs on Canadian trusts)

6. Foreign utility company ETFs

7. Foreign currency certificates of deposit

If you still have money to invest, you can add:

1. Foreign currency ETFs

2. Gold mining ETFs

3. Gold ETF

4. GoldMoney or other trustworthy digital gold currency

5. Commodity ETFs

If you are frightened of an economic apocalypse, keep some small gold coins or bars at home in your safe.

(However, if you think we could be as bad off as post-war Japan, canned goods and soap might be more valuable.)

If a variable annuity is right for you (see your financial adviser), consider a Swiss annuity.

You can't invest in all of these unless you're wealthy. Pick what's right for you, buy what you can now, and add to your portfolio as time goes by. That includes using income from your portfolio as well as your income from your job or business.

Always reinvest portfolio income unless you need it to live on. That's how to become wealthy.

This is the end of the type of information you probably expected to get out of this book.

Overwhelmed? I don't blame you.

See the next chapter for one single investment to protect your US dollar purchasing power.

Chapter 18

Keeping It Simple

If you have at least $2,000 but not enough to diversify with many of the investments listed in the prior chapter, there's one mutual fund created especially for US dollar bears.

Most of its holdings are short-term sovereign notes and bills. It does include some U.S. fixed income investments, and gold and gold stocks.

Countries represented have included (this can vary): Singapore, Japan, Sweden, Norway, Canada, Hong Kong, Denmark, and the Netherlands.

This is undoubtedly the best "one-stop shopping" ways to protect your US dollar purchasing power.

The one scenario it doesn't prepare you for is a crushing deflationary depression that lowers the price of gold and makes all these governments default on their debts.

Because it's a mutual fund, it's also suitable if you wish to make small investments over time. They do have a Systematic Investment Program to help you do that.

Federated Prudent Dollar Bear Fund — formerly Federated Prudent Global Income Fund — **(PSAFX)**

Expense ratio: 1.30%. Dividends are paid annually. 30.45 cents in 2010.

The breakdown of its current holdings:

Invests in Non-U. S. fixed income - 87.3%

U.S. fixed income — 8.1%

Gold and gold stocks — 4.6%

But your 3 step program not protect your US dollar is not complete yet.

This only completes Step 1.

Protecting your purchasing power is not just about the value of the US dollar. Stop throwing away US dollars.

Chapter 19

Get Out of Debt and Control Your Spending

I'm not an expert on these subjects, but I feel I'd be remiss if I failed to mention them.

To me, you shouldn't get upset about the value of the US dollar going down against the euro or yen if you yourself are throwing away your purchasing power.

Stop wasting your US dollars on interest payments, wasted food, unnecessary shopping and so on.

When it comes to getting out of debt, Dave Ramsey is the preacher you need to listen to. I'm now not working when his radio show is on, but I used to hear it a lot, and enjoyed hearing people scream, "I'm debt freeeeeeeee!!!" on the air.

It takes guts, stubbornness, patience and self-sacrifice, but do it anyway.

Another radio show host is a master at saving money — Clark Howard.

Do you really need to pay $10 for the latest movie in a theater when it's going to be shown on cable and satellite TV in three to six months?

Do you really need the fastest speed of DSL service?

Do you really need a gym membership? You can do pushups anywhere you have empty floor space.

Do you really need the latest smart cell phone?

Could you find a car insurance company that'll give you the same coverage for less money?

How about cutting down on the junk food you buy? I'm tired of going into my local gas station and hearing people gripe about the cost of gasoline while they're holding ten dollars' worth of hot dogs, snack cakes and 128 ounce sodas, and when they reach the counter add a carton of cigarettes and ten lottery quick pick tickets. You'll be healthier and lighter as well as wealthier.

If you smoke, stop. I know it's not easy. Do you want to own a lot of US dollars or do you want to literally burn them up to poison your lungs?

If you go to Vegas or local casinos, or gamble online — stop.

I know the odds. Unless you're a kick ass poker player, sports bettor or horse bettor — and those are rarer than you think — you're a loser.

Here's Your Action Plan

Sit down with your partner or by yourself if you live alone, and list everything you spend your money on, and how much it costs you every month.

Cable or satellite TV.

Food.

Rent or mortgage

and so on.

Think long and hard. You probably don't realize how much you're spending on some items, such as food, so estimate as well as you can.

Then go through every item and ask yourself whether it's really necessary.

If not, stop wasting money on it.

For necessities, such as food, ask yourself how you can reduce what you're spending. Take sandwiches to work instead of going out. Fry your own hamburgers instead of stopping at the Golden Arches.

Sell your expensive late model SUV and buy an eight year old four cylinder that'll still get you to work.

If you're living in a house now too expensive for you, take steps to downsize. I know it's not easy to sell houses these days,

Richard Stooker

especially if you owe more than it's now worth. If you can afford to stay in it and your local area is still a buyer's market — but there are no buyers — you may be better off waiting a year or two (or three).

I guarantee you can find many ways to cut back and cut down on what you're spending.

Make a Budget and Stick to It

It's not fun, but the more you do it the better you'll feel. You'll feel good you're more in control of your life. You'll feel good you're not being ripped off or just plain flushing money down the toilet.

Once you've figured out how to cut your expenses to the necessities, organize them into a monthly and weekly budget.

This includes listing your separate debts in the order in which it'd be best to pay them off.

Your more "flexible" bills, such as credit cards come first. List them in order of the interest rate they're charging you, the highest ones first.

If some are charging you essentially the same interest rate, put the one with the lower balance first.

You must pay the minimum balance on all of them every month to keep your credit score intact.

However, apply all extra money to the one bill you've targeted to pay off first.

When it's paid off, go down the list.

After you've paid off all those, save the extra money every month until you have enough to pay off the balance of fixed loans such as your car.

And yes, the final step is to pay off your mortgage.

Until You Can Pay the Entire Balance, Make the Required Monthly Payments and Keep The Rest in a Savings or Money Market Account

It's possible to add extra money to the check you write your mortgage company every month and — in theory — you're paying off your principal balance faster.

However, I've heard mortgage companies don't deal well with that. You cannot depend on them to be giving you credit for that extra money.

In theory, every time you pay something extra on your mortgage, the amortization schedule of monthly principal and interest should be adjusted, so with every future payment you're paying slightly more principal and slightly less interest.

However, you can't count on this.

There are services that will make or keep track of your extra payments — and how they should modify your mortgage — for you. But they usually have a system whereby you're still paying a fixed amount which is a "thirteenth" monthly payment for the year. What if something happens and you can't do that? What if you want to pay a lot more than that?

There's an additional problem if you do this, even if the mortgage company accounting gives you accurate credit for your extra payments.

You cannot access that money again if you have a financial emergency.

Yes, it counts as part of the principal you have in your home, but if you're out of work or out of business you'll have trouble getting a home equity loan.

And most of all, why pay a service a lot of money when it's not necessary?

Just do it yourself.

Open up a money market account for this purpose. Every month, put all the extra money you can into it. Don't touch it (unless you have a financial emergency) until the balance is high enough to pay off your home loan.

Once you stop throwing away so many US dollars, you can focus on increasing your spending power by increasing your US dollar income.

Chapter 19

Make More Money

I'd also feel remiss if I fail to point out another powerful way to increase the purchasing power of your supply of US dollars is to increase the number of US dollars you have coming in.

You can start by going through your house and selling everything you don't need. I bet you'll find a lot more stuff than you think.

The clothes that no longer fit you. The clothes that no longer fit your children. The toys they're now too old to play with. The books you're never going to read again. The DVDs you're never going to watch again.

For things that are currently sold on Amazon, you can sign up for a sellers' account (scroll to the bottom of their home page and look under the "Make Money With Us" section. First link under us says "Sell on Amazon." Click there. It's free to sign up and list items.

There is a charge, of course, but you don't pay it until the item is sold. Then Amazon will take their fee out of what the buyer pays.

You do need a product number. This is hard for most products, but easy for books, CDs and DVDs. If you look at their bar codes, you'll see their ISBN. You list it by that ISBN.

It must be an item Amazon is currently selling anyway. If it's too old or not for sale on Amazon, you must go to eBay or Craigslist.

eBay is for selling items older, rarer and worth more.

For items too common or ordinary for Amazon or eBay or Craigslist, hold a garage sale.

Take a second job.

Work all available overtime.

Put in for a promotion.

Find a service to sell online (see the next chapter for expats)

Take certification classes.

Go back to college to get a degree or a higher degree.

Apply for better jobs than you have now.

Buy a fixer upper house in a good neighborhood, fix it up yourself and rent it out.

Start some kind of home business.

I don't know you so I don't know what's best for you and your family, but I guarantee you already know how to do something useful to make extra money — or you can learn.

I guarantee unless you're already following one of these suggestions, there's time in your life you could turn into money.

The average American watches TV six hours a day then complains they don't have time to do what they want. Somebody's watching TV twelve hours a day because I watch 0 hours!

When it comes to thriving during the coming dollar crash, remember Robert Lichello's story about post-war Japan. Hopefully we'll never have to live through a time when our country is massively, physically damaged.

The main point was, people first of all want to meet their basic needs: food, clothing and shelter. Safety and comfort.

If you're a computer programmer you can take steps to make more money in your career, perhaps through getting certified, or learning new languages and techniques, or taking project management training so you can move up into management, or writing iPhone and Facebook apps in the evening, either for yourself or for hire.

That's great for now. But you might also consider raising vegetables or something else that would be useful and in demand when your neighbors are too busy thinking about surviving the night to care about electronic gadgets.

But maybe you're not living inside the United States right now.

Maybe you're on the front lines of the US dollar war. Maybe you're an expatriate.

Chapter 20

For Expatriates

The people on the "front lines" of the battle to defend the US dollar are expats.

I know it can be tough.

I can't give much specific advice. A lot depends on your age, your abilities, what country you're in and so on.

If you live on the Left Bank of Paris you have different challenges than if you're in a shack in rural Indonesia.

There're a lot of books on the subject in general, and if you're already living in another country you know more about it than I do.

If you're not already married/partnered, I'd suggest — for your financial safety — you avoid any romantic relationships with the locals.

And no, I couldn't take that advice either!

However, I do encourage you to go through this 3 step process.

1. Go through the budgeting I describe in Chapter 17. Figure out where you can save money. Maybe you don't really need that fancy beach villa and the cook and the gardener. Maybe you could live just fine in a smaller house two blocks away from the ocean.

If you're in Japan or Spain, maybe you should consider moving to a cheaper country. Thailand or Croatia.

2. Go through the make more money ideas I describe in Chapter 18.

Do a thorough evaluation of your knowledge and skills. Chances are good you know how to do something somebody else will pay you for.

If it's only speaking and writing English, take a Teaching English as a Second Language (TESL) course and get a local teaching job or offer private tutoring. In many areas you don't need a TESL certificate, especially if you simply tutor people privately.

It's now possible to sell an enormous range of services online.

Teach high school or college courses — yes, online.

Write articles, reports, websites, emails or entire books. The biggest money is in copywriting — that is, writing to make sales. However, many people make good money writing other types of material, including business marketing. Local businesses may be glad to pay you to write a website in English.

If you're artistic, do graphic design work.

Virtual assistants handle a lot of routine business work for distant clients.

Submit websites to directories. Write Twitter posts. Social bookmarking — there are a lot of routine services webmasters and Internet marketers need done which they're glad to outsource.

Once you have too many clients to handle the chores yourself, find local high school or college students to take the grunt work out of your hands while you search for more clients.

For many ideas on how you can make money online or for services you can outsource to Internet marketers, visit the WarriorForum.com and spend a lot of time reading it.

Incidentally, marketing online can be another way to hedge your currency risk. That's because you might work for someone in any country. Which means you might get paid in any currency. If you can make a Belgium online marketer happy, they'll keep paying you in euros.

You can handle such transactions in most of the world through Pay Pal.

If you're knowledgeable about business, you can give speeches and presentations to local business organization. Make those free, but promote your consulting services.

Or give specialized seminars. There are an incredible number of organizations promoting specific skills, from reiki to yoga to speed reading to childhood development to business communications to neurolinguistic programming.

Find something you're interested in, go to the seminar yourself and get certified to teach it, then give such seminars in your local area, or teach the skill through tutoring.

3. Go through the investing options I describe in the bulk of this book and summarize in Chapter 16.

Focus on what most applies to you. If you're living in Germany, obviously you need to focus on protecting yourself against a rising euro.

Invest what you have as well as possible, given all the options and how big your portfolio is.

If you're thinking about owning physical gold bars or coins, be careful. Check out your local laws first. And make sure you keep it well hidden. If you're not sure you can trust local gold dealers, don't. I have no doubt in some countries in some neighborhoods, the gold dealers are in cahoots with local burglars, especially regarding "wealthy" foreigners.

Obviously you can open a savings account in your local bank that pays interest — but is it enough to keep up with the cost of living in your area? If you're in a small country that can't afford to track its own inflation, you may not know.

If you've already paid for your home, so food and utilities are your biggest necessary expenses and your income is substantial, it may not be worth stressing out about.

However, I suggest you put some money into a third currency

(that is, not the US dollar and not your local currency) from another continent, as a form of hedging and insurance.

For example, if you're living in Korea, keep some money in a euro certificate of deposit through Everbank. That way you have some protection in case both the US dollar and the won crash.

No matter where you live, invest in some foreign stocks and bonds ETFs. This will give you a broad base of currency diversification.

Chapter 21

Reduced Spending Power is Better Than Zero Spending Power

During times of high inflation, many financial advisers recommend people spend their money before it loses more spending power. I heard that a lot during the 1970s.

Thinking about buying a new TV? Better get it now, before the price goes up.

Don't save your money, was typical advice. It'll go down in value.

I believe this is misguided and dangerous.

Here's an example.

A married couple have saved up $10,000. They're debating whether to put it into a certificate of deposit to keep for their retirement or whether to take a long cruise around the world.

If they save that $10,000, inflation will decrease its purchasing power. By the time they retire, it's worth only enough to buy hamburger instead of dog meat.

Should they sail around the world because a cruise is worth a lot more than hamburger?

Or should they keep the money, because hamburger is so much better to eat than dog food?

Hamburger seems to be worth a lot less than a world cruise, but when you're sick and elderly and your alternative is eating dog food, it's extremely valuable.

Now, you can argue the cruise will enrich their relationship and give them wonderful memories for their lifetimes, and that's fine.

If you go on the cruise, go on it for cruise-related reasons.

Don't spend the money just because you have money in your hand and everybody is telling you to spend it.

Go on the cruise if and only if you really want that cruise, and can afford it – and still save money for retirement.

Even during inflation, you should save money.

You should be smart about in what form you save it — that's what this book is all about. Maybe you could take that certificate of deposit out in Swiss francs instead of US dollars.

But you should certainly save as much money as you can.

I'm not your financial adviser, but if that $10,000 is all the excess money you have, you can't afford a cruise.

And what if we suffer deflation instead of inflation?

During a depression, cash is king. You might go on that cruise for half or more off today's price.

Chapter 22

Wrapping Up

There you have it — my simple 3 step plan to protect your US dollar purchasing power.

1. Cut your expenses and debt.

2. Increase your income.

3. Make a wide range of foreign currency and income producing investments.

If you can afford to and you're afraid of total economic collapse (I don't believe it will happen but I can't promise you it won't), have some gold coins and bars on hand.

By now, you may be shaking your head.

Maybe you've noticed something interesting.

With one modification, this 3 step plan is a terrific process for EVERYBODY to secure their financial future.

That modification is...along with buying foreign currency

investments, include US dollar, income producing investments.

U.S. consumer brands that pay dividends.

U.S. corporate and Treasury bonds, including TIPS.

U.S. REITs.

U.S. utilities.

That way, you're diversified against the risk sometime in the future Western Europe and Japan both collapse while the United States remains strong. Remember, both the Eurozone and Japan have significant demographic problems. They're both growing old. They're not replacing their dead with enough babies.

The United States still has a higher than replacement birth rate. We also are allowing in new immigrants, which Japan does not. To be Japanese, you have to be born Japanese.

Europe is allowing in immigrants, but for the most part it's keeping them isolated. That's why a few years ago France had riots of Muslim youth. Those were probably caused more by economic frustration than by religious extremism. In the U.S. most of them would be working at Taco Bell and going to college.

We're experiencing social dislocation but, to a far larger degree than Europe, we're assimilating immigrants.

As I wrote earlier, I do believe our economic situation must get a lot worse before we as a country force our politicians to be fiscally responsible. But there are signs the process has begun.

A lot of people reacted negatively to the Republican-Democrat stand-off over the debt deal leading up to August 2.

I want us to cut the budget more, but I think the whole situation was a positive one.

Now the country is talking about how to cut the budget. Until recently, Congress raised the debt ceiling without a blink. Now it's big news story.

Now we're debating it.

If Greek politicians had had this fight five years ago, they might not have had austerity forced on them, along with blood in the streets over it.

Now it's time for you to get your own financial house in order.

So get started already.

The End

Special Offer for Readers of Bring on the Crash!

To thank you, I want to give you my new report The Death of Capital Gains.

The longest bull market in history peaked in October 2007.

The last twelve years have been a "lost dozen" where the Dow Jones is back to where it was many years ago.
Thousands of Americans are in city parks whining the stock market is a scam and capitalism no longer works.
The old paradigms have shifted.

Where're the 10% average annual gains the experts promised the stock market would deliver?

If you plan to retire someday, you need to learn where the real stock market wealth is today.

If you think some pension or mutual fund manager knows how to beat the market, or some TV or newsletter guru, you better get wise quick.

If you believe you can discover undervalued stocks by reading annual reports or monitoring Yahoo! Finance, you better get real.

The world economic and financial systems are teetering. The people, businesses, state and local governments, and national governments of the world have dug a huge hole of debt.

Nobody knows what's going to happen. When a rating agency can downgrade the United States government, nobody knows what else the future may bring.

Greeks are rioting in Athens and Americans in Oakland California.

Still think all you have to do to be set for life is find some low "P/E" stocks?

We're in the early stages of a monster bear market. The old strategies won't work.

Yet the new ones are not magical or even complicated.
Learn about the problem—and the solution—in The Death of Capital Gains investing.

Just go to this web page:

http://www.incomeinvesthome.com/free/